MODERN CONTAINER GARDENING

Isabelle Palmer

How to Create
a Stylish Small-space
Garden Anywhere

Hardie Grant

BOOKS

Contents

GETTING STARTED

My Gardening Journey

It all started with one pot on a balcony; soon there were ten, and then 30! From a simple desire to make the most of my small outdoor space, I'd soon created a container garden where I could sit and enjoy plants in the city.

So, what's this book about? Well, it's aimed first and foremost at helping you to begin a container garden from scratch, albeit in just one pot or a collection of planters. You may know very little about gardening – and have no idea where to begin – so it sets out to teach you the basics. I hope it will also provide you with inspiration and ideas for your containers, whether you are a complete novice or a seasoned gardener.

If you are lacking in gardening experience, then my best advice is to start small with just a few containers of low-maintenance plants that are easy to care for. Once you understand that plants are just living things which require water, food and light, some care and attention, and the right location in which to thrive, I'm sure you will be bitten by the gardening bug. Armed with more horticultural knowledge, you can then expand your retinue, space permitting, with plants that you love and which will fill you with a sense of pride and enjoyment. To me that's gardening in a nutshell.

As much as possible, I've tried to avoid bamboozling you with Latin terminology for the names of plants, which I think can make some people afraid of gardening. They also make gardening seem far more complicated than it actually is. Due to the complexities of the world of botany, plants are known by their Latin names, with common names often varying from country to country, and often region to region within those countries. For this reason, I've provided the Latin names of the plants in each of the projects, to ensure you can track down the right ones. Throughout the rest of the book, I've used the plants' most familiar or popular common names as appropriate. Feel free to Google the plants – it only takes a second and you'll often find yourself discovering other cultivars and varieties that really appeal to you and inspire ideas for new planters.

Perhaps one of the most important aspects of container gardening is that you can grow plants in seemingly impossible places. You are also not committed to a whole garden, whether you have one or not, and you can take your plants with you if you move. I have had many specimens come along for the ride with me all over London and have not had to say goodbye to my favourites, which gives me all the more reason to have a garden in containers.

I have tried to include ideas for planters that will appeal to a wide variety of tastes, including a cool, sophisticated display of shade-loving plants in a pair of concrete containers, a collection of pretty, cottage-garden flowers in large planters, and some climber-clad trellis in a large copper trough that's perfect for brightening up a courtyard. Where practical, I've organised the projects according to their main season of interest, although obviously there will be some overlap between seasons, as well as differences depending on where in the world you're gardening. For example, although the initial flush of colour and drama in a particular container may be over by the end of summer, you'll find that some of the plants will continue to put on a fabulous display beyond this time, and so extending the season of interest.

My goal in writing this book is to equip you with the basics for growing plants in containers so you will hopefully understand a little more about gardening and how to navigate some unfamiliar horticultural terminology (there is a glossary of gardening terms on page 14–15). That knowledge may grow in time, or maybe it won't. However, that doesn't matter because, for me, gardening is not about learning information to take an exam; it's about fulfilment and enjoyment.

In short, I've tried to create the book that I wish I'd had years ago when I first started out in container gardening. I hope you enjoy the journey as much as I have.

— *Isabelle*

How to Use This Book

My aim with this book is to provide an all-round, easy-to-understand guide to container gardening, whether you are a complete novice or have some gardening experience.

To start you off, I've included a helpful how-to guide that covers the basics. There you will find advice on the type of equipment you'll need, on choosing containers, and on selecting plants. I also guide you through working out the growing conditions in your outdoor space so you can be sure of selecting plants that are likely to thrive – and therefore sustain your success and confidence! There is useful information on planting mediums to ensure your new plants get off to the best start. Once you have the foundations in place – the right container, the best potting mix, and the most suitable plants for your growing conditions – you'll be well on your way to keeping your plants fit and healthy.

I have covered the most basic starting points, including how to read a plant label and how to work out what direction your site faces in. These are questions that I was baffled by at the start, so I wanted to explain these here. To ensure continued success, the how-to section also gives instructions about preparing your containers and plants before planting, along with step-by-step sequences that demonstrate the best techniques for potting up.

Once you've planted your containers with gorgeous planting schemes, it would be a shame for all your hard work to go to waste through inadequate care and maintenance, so I guide your through this,

too, providing advice on watering and feeding; keeping plants neat and tidy; and how to deal with the pests, diseases and disorders that all gardeners inevitably face at some stage. I'll point out here, however, that of all the maintenance tasks required for successful container gardening, the single most important thing you can do for your plants is to water them regularly and consistently. Along with feeding, this is the key to flourishing container plants – they are utterly dependent on you for their moisture and nutrient needs, so please take the time to read this practical section carefully.

The projects are organised by season – spring or late spring and early summer, for example. Then, to keep things simple, I have devised a set of symbols that appear with each project. You can discover what these symbols mean on page 55. Each project is given a difficulty rating; you'll find that most are easy and suitable for the complete novice. If you are unsure, start with a single container with a few annual plants that you love and build up from there to more complex projects containing permanent plantings of shrubs and climbers, for example. The symbols are also used to highlight the best aspect for each project (that is, whether the plants listed require full sun or partial shade), as well as an indication of their watering and feeding requirements. They also give a rough guide to the container's main season of interest, but I should point out that this will vary according to where in the world you are gardening – you may find the plants flower for longer or shorter

periods in your area, depending on local conditions, so please bear this in mind.

In an attempt to make things as straightforward as possible, I have provided a list with each project of the tools and equipment you'll need. These lists include details on the paints necessary to replicate the finish on the container, although please feel free to choose different colours to suit your home and personal tastes. Where possible, I've also given a rough indication of the size of the container used for each project and accompanied this with a 'shopping list' of plants (including numbers used) which will grow well in a container of that size. However, as your confidence grows and you discover more plants, you will be able to use the projects as a springboard for your own ideas and planting schemes.

I should add a note of caution here, though: although most plants can be grown in containers, be aware that larger plants such as small trees and shrubs, grasses and ferns, which are happy confined to a pot for a season or two, will probably need transplanting to the open garden or potting up into a much larger container at the very least. Unless they are true container plants (such as annual bedding plants and tender perennials), they will be under stress if grown long-term in a container. If you are unable to transplant them in the garden, I suggest you pass them to a friend or family member who has the space to accommodate them. I have found over the years that plants make excellent gifts.

The step-by-step instructions then explain the best way to prepare and plant up each container. Coupled with useful notes and tips on caring for the containers once planted, my intention is to equip you with everything you need to make your foray into container gardening a success.

Tools and Equipment

Growing plants in containers calls for a few tools and pieces of equipment, many of which are the same as you would use in the open garden. Here I look at some of the most important items you'll need.

Hand Tools

A hand trowel and hand fork will prove invaluable. You can use a hand trowel to dig potting mix and add additives such as horticultural sand, grit, perlite and vermiculite (see pages 28–29). A hand fork is useful for breaking up potting mix and working fertiliser granules into the top layer of potting mix, for example. Plastic or metal potting mix scoops in a range of sizes can be used for measuring – large scoops hold more potting mix than a trowel and make it easier to pot up. If you are short of space, then Burgon & Ball supply an excellent range of container-focused tools. The Container Root and Transplanting Knife are good replacements for a hand trowel and fork.

Equipment for Watering

Perhaps the most important piece of equipment for the container gardener is a watering can. I suggest using a fine rose attachment for watering plants with delicate leaves. If you are using a liquid fertiliser, then you can apply this directly to the potting mix without using the rose. Large containers with permanent plantings of trees and shrubs, for example, can be watered with a garden hose if you have one. I tend to go for larger watering cans because that means fewer trips to fill up, but a small watering can will do too.

Gardening Gloves

It is advisable to wear a pair of gardening gloves when handling potting mix or plants with thorns (this also saves your nails). You may also want to wear gloves when applying fertilisers or commercial products for controlling pests and diseases. I use a tight-fitting rubber indoor pair that make the job much easier.

Tools for Cutting

A good pair of secateurs is essential for pruning shrubs and generally tidying up container plants. A sharp pair of scissors is great for deadheading plants as well.

Tip — Keep your tools clean and they will last much longer – just rinse and dry them after use. Secateurs and scissors should also be cleaned after use to stop them rusting and to keep the blades nice and sharp.

USEFUL TOOLS AND EQUIPMENT

Hand trowel

Hand fork

Plastic or metal scoop

Dustpan and brush (very handy for potting and cleaning up fallen foliage)

Rolls of rubbish bags

Large plastic tray (for measuring out potting mix and mixing in additives)

Bucket (optional)

Watering can (with a fine rose attachment)

Garden hose (for watering trees and shrubs)

Secateurs

Sharp scissors

Gardening gloves

Electric drill or a hammer and heavy-duty nail (for putting drainages holes in containers)

Galvanised garden wire

Vine eyes

HELPFUL EXTRAS

Plant labels and a waterproof pen

Garden canes or pea sticks (to stake taller plants)

Garden twine, string or raffia

Pot mover on wheels for relocating large planters

Gardening Terms

The following is a glossary of terms that you might find helpful – it is by no means exhaustive and primarily tailored to container gardening.

Acidic   Acidic soils and potting mixes have a pH between zero and seven. Ericaceous potting mixes suitable for acid-loving plants such as heathers and azaleas are available.

Alkaline   Alkaline soils have a pH of more than seven and are often described as chalky. They can make it tricky for plants to absorb some nutrients. Always check plant and soil combinations before planting to make sure they are the right fit.

Annual   A plant that completes its life cycle (i.e. blooms, produces seed and dies) in one year.

Bedding plant   Fast-growing, usually colourful plants (annuals and tender perennials) grown in beds and containers for summer. Usually thrown away at the end of the growing season.

Biennial   A plant that has a two-year life cycle, producing leaves in the first year and flowers in the second.

Bolting   Usually the result of excessive heat and sun exposure, bolting occurs when a plant produces premature flowers or seeds instead of a crop.

Botanical name   The scientific name of a plant, consisting of the genus (always capitalised) and species (not capitalised) – for example, *Lavandula angustifolia* (English lavender). Some plants have further parts to their names: the variety, or cultivar.

Bulb   Plants with fleshy underground storage organs (for example, daffodils and tulips).

Climber   A plant that will grow and creep over trellis and other similar structures.

Coir   A composted organic material made from coconut fibre. Often used as a substitute for peat in soil-less potting mixes.

Cultivar   A plant bred or selected by nurseries for its unique attributes, such as flowers and leaf colour, making it different to the original species. It is a cultivated variety rather than a naturally occurring variety of the plant.

Cut back   Trimming or clipping plants to encourage new growth.

Deadheading   The removal of dead and faded flowers in order to encourage further flushes of flowers and prevent seeding.

Deciduous   A plant that loses its leaves each year.

Drainage   The movement of water through soil/potting mix. Good drainage is important to avoid root rot.

Ericaceous   A term used to describe plants that prefer acidic soils or potting mix. They will not tolerate alkaline soils (i.e. those that contain lime or chalk).

Evergreen   A plant that keeps its leaves throughout the growing season. Examples include pittosporum and box.

Fertiliser   An organic or synthetic material, usually in either granular or liquid form, used to feed plants.

Foliar feed   Feeding plants by applying a liquid fertiliser directly to the leaves (following the manufacturer's directions).

Frost   Occurs when moisture in the air condenses and freezes. Tender plants, as well as those grown in containers, are at a high risk of damage from frost and cold temperatures.

Fungicide   A type of pesticide used to kill and control the spread of fungi.

Hardy   Plants (often evergreens) that can withstand exposure to frost and temperatures down to -15°C (5°F) without damage to their leaves. Some plants are half-hardy, meaning they can be grown outdoors, but require winter protection from frost and temperatures below 0°C (32°F).

Herbicide   A substance used to kill plants (usually weeds) or inhibit plant growth.

Hybrid   A plant variety resulting from the crossing of two different genera or species.

Insecticide   A type of pesticide used to kill or deter insects.

Invasive   A plant that spreads quickly, crowding out other plants, and is difficult to control.

Mulch   A material such as bark chips that is spread over the surface of soil and potting mix to help retain moisture and control weeds. Often referred to as a decorative trim for containers, examples include gravel and slate.

NPK   An abbreviation of the three main nutrients (known as macronutrients) required by plants – nitrogen (N), phosphorus (P) and potassium (K). Fertiliser labels usually display how much of each macronutrient the product contains.

Ornamental   Plants grown for the way they look, rather than for consumption or economic uses.

Peat   Remains of dead bog plants or moss that are nutrient-rich and retain water well. Peat is removed from peat bogs for use in some potting mixes, which is considered environmentally unfriendly. Peat-substitute-based potting mixes are also available.

Perennial   A plant that lives and flowers for more than two growing seasons. They are either evergreens or die back in winter before flowering again the following year.

Pendent   Used to describe flowers, leaves or branches that hang down (rather than being upright).

Perlite   A naturally occurring, white volcanic glass that can be incorporated into potting mix to improve drainage while also maintaining moisture levels.

Pesticide   A chemical compound used to kill pests, fungi and unwanted weeds.

Potbound   A term used to describe when the roots of a container-grown plant have run out of room. Roots are sometimes seen growing out of the holes in the base of the container.

Potting mix   A packaged soil mixture for growing container plants. It can contain sterilised loam (soil), peat, sharp sand and fertilisers. Some potting mixes do not contain any soil (being based on peat or peat substitutes like coir fibre). Specialist mixes are also available for different plant groups such as cacti and succulents.

Potting on   Planting a container-grown plant in the next pot size up.

Pruning   The removal of dead, damaged or diseased branches and foliage. Pruning is often carried out for ornamental reasons such as topiary.

Root ball   A plant's root system surrounded by soil.

Seedling   A plant that has just emerged from its seed or germinated.

Shrub   A woody plant, either evergreen or deciduous, with a framework of branches.

Specimen plant   A plant, often a tree or shrub, grown in a prominent position in a garden or container.

Starter plant   A small plant seedling (often called a plug plant) that is grown in an individual cell for planting in a container or directly in the ground.

Succulent   Plants with stems and/or leaves that are fleshy, thick and watery. Often waxy to allow the succulent to retain water well.

Tender   Used to describe a plant's inability to survive cold temperatures and frost. Tender perennials such as pelargoniums can be overwintered under cover.

Top-dress   Providing a container plant with fresh nutrients by removing the top layer of potting mix and adding fresh potting mix or fertilisers.

Topiary   Creating different shapes from woody plants through clipping and training.

Trailing   A plant that produces long stems along the ground, often rooting as they grow, which can be used in containers to trail down over the sides.

Variegated   Plants with leaves that are patterned with different colours (usually whites, creams and yellows).

Variety   A term used in plant classification to identify a variation in a species.

Vermiculite   An expanded mineral, usually grey or beige, which is added to potting mix to improve drainage while still helping retain water.

Weed   A plant with no value in a garden or container that grows where it is not wanted.

THE
BASICS

Choosing Plants

You can grow most plants in containers that you would grow in the open garden. Container plants come in a wide range of shapes, sizes and colours and include small trees (such as purple beech), shrubs (such as pittosporum, phormiums and cordylines), climbers (such as clematis and sweet peas), as well as perennials, grasses, bulbs and annual bedding plants.

To ensure success, ascertain whether you can provide your choice of plants with the right growing conditions. You can easily supply the best growing medium, but the amount of light your outdoor space receives is beyond your control. The level of sunshine is by far the most important factor for ensuring your plants will thrive – some plants like lots of sun, others don't, so try to choose plants that will grow well in your space. The amount of sunshine a space receives depends on the 'aspect'. This is the direction in which your garden faces – whether this is north, south, east or west. This affects which areas get lots of sun and which ones are in the shade for all or part of the day.

So, first of all, work out whether you have a sunny or shady aspect, and tailor your planting to the available light.

Working Out the Aspect of Your Space

You may have heard people comment joyously that they have a south-facing garden, but why is this important? When I started my first containers, I was unsure of this, so I will explain here. Using the compass on your smartphone, stand outside with your back to your property and facing your garden, balcony, etc. Whatever position is directly ahead of you is the position your garden faces. So, if south is ahead of you, then your garden is south-facing. The following summarises the light levels in gardens with different aspects:

South-facing gardens receive the most sunlight

West-facing gardens receive afternoon and evening light

East-facing gardens receive morning light

North-facing gardens receive the least light

Sun Versus Shade – Which is Better?

Strictly speaking, all aspects have pros and cons in terms
of container gardening. Yes, there are more plants that prefer
lots of sunshine – and who doesn't want a sunny garden –
but that also means you will have to water your containers
more frequently. There are a few tricks you can employ to
offset low light levels. For instance, to reflect light back into
a space, try painting walls in white or cream, using mirrors
and adding pale reflective gravel mulches. These techniques
will trick plants into thinking they're somewhere sunnier.

If you're gardening up high on a balcony or roof garden,
then the wind factor also plays a part. Drying winds can
desiccate plants, so bear this in mind when making your
selection. You can also grow evergreen screening plants such
as golden bamboo and laurel in large planters to provide
shelter from cold, drying winds for susceptible plants.

Buying Your Plants – Where to Start?

I suggest you do a little bit of research and make notes before you buy any plants. This is the best approach for gaining a clearer idea of what you need, so you don't stand dumbfounded in the garden centre not knowing where to start – which I have done at times.

I advise you to buy your containers first. This may seem a little odd, but it's the best place to begin. Starting with the containers means that you can decide how much space you want to fill, where to put them and then how many plants you need to get. For advice on choosing containers, see pages 22–23. If you buy the containers before the plants, it's a good idea to take them with you to the plant nursery or garden centre. If that's not possible, make sure you at least take a picture of them on your phone. That way, you can match the containers to your selection of plants.

If you're choosing plants for the first time, I suggest always going to the nursery or garden centre in person. Although you can buy plants online, for me one of the most enjoyable parts of gardening is looking at and choosing them. That aside, it's imperative to see the array of colour in the shopping trolley so you can check you're happy with the combinations. The plants are going to become part of your home, so you want to get this right. It's also important to pick the healthiest plants in order to give your containers the best possible start, which sometimes doesn't happen with online purchases, believe me.

Most plant nurseries and garden centres will have someone there who can help you out, so don't be afraid to ask. Typically, the plants are organised and labelled according to how much sun they require and which plants like shade to give you a starting point and guide you if you're unsure of what to get.

How to Choose Healthy Plants

Even though plants may be cheaper online, it's worth selecting your own at a nursery or garden centre to ensure you're buying the healthiest specimens. Here is a useful checklist of what to look out for:

Plant health — check for signs of pests and diseases. The eggs of insects, for example, are often attached to the undersides of leaves, so look over the foliage carefully.

Root system — if possible, remove the plant from its plastic pot and inspect the roots. They should be firm and look healthy. A plant that is pot-bound, with a mass of tangled roots growing out of the bottom of the plastic pot, is best avoided.

Leaves and flowers — make sure these look healthy, without any discoloration or markings.

Flowering plants — choose plants that have lots of unopened buds. That way, you know you'll get great value, particularly from annual bedding plants.

Plants Sometimes Die – Don't worry: Keep Calm and Carry On

Even the most experienced gardeners have times when their plants fail to thrive and even die. If rehabilitation, pruning, watering and feeding, and pest and disease remedies don't work, then I'm afraid it is more sensible to throw the plant away and start again. It is an excuse to visit the garden centre, and buy more plants, so don't feel defeated. Gardening is all about learning from your mistakes and moving on. Apart from anything else, if a plant in a container is diseased, then it is better to pull it out before it infects other specimens.

How to Read a Plant Label

Below is an example of a typical plant label, with a more in-depth description of the details they often give in the chart below.

COLUMBINE
Aquilegia vulgaris

Full sun/partial shade
60–80 cm (24–32 in)

FRONT

This showy herbaceous perennial produces delicate blue flowers. Ideal for containers and cut flowers.

Water ◊ ◊ ◊

Habit Upright/tall

Position Full sun or partial shade

Blooms Early summer or autumn

Spacing 20 cm (8 in)

Hardiness Frost hardy

Fertilisation Monthly

BACK

FRONT

Common Name
Columbine

Botanical Name
Plant's genus, species and variety/cultivar (as appropriate)

Sun requirements
How much sun the plant needs to grow well

Height
How tall you can expect the plant to grow

QR code
Scan this on a smartphone for further information on the plant

Uses
Guideline on how to use the plant

Water
◊   Let the soil dry out between waterings
◊◊   Let the soil dry an inch or so at the top between waterings
◊◊◊   Keep the soil moist constantly

Habit
The shape in which the plant grows (i.e. upright, mounding or trailing)

Blooms
When the plant flowers

BACK

Position
How much sun or shade is required:

Full sun	6+ hours direct sun per day
Partial shade	4–6 hours direct sun per day
Full shade	Less than 4 hours direct sun per day

Spacing
How much space to leave between plants (this can be reduced slightly in containers)

Hardiness
Ability to withstand harsh conditions

Fertilise
How often to fertilise

Choosing Containers

Container gardening is not confined to small spaces, such as courtyards, balconies and roof gardens, or to urban areas either for that matter. Admittedly, if you only have a small balcony, then a few containers allow you to indulge your horticultural passion and enjoy plants throughout the year, but larger gardens can also benefit from some well-chosen containers.

There is a wide range of containers available made from traditional terracotta, concrete and zinc in many different sizes and materials. You can also recycle items to produce a display that's uniquely yours. Your local garden centre will have a good selection to choose from, and you'll also find a fantastic choice online. Take the time to consider the sizes, shapes, colours and prices. Putting containers together to create a 'garden' is a real opportunity to experiment with different textures and shades. Inevitably, the containers you choose will be dictated by the amount of space you have, as well as by personal preference and budget. However, I think it's better to buy a couple of key containers than lots of smaller ones.

Don't forget the importance of matching the style/material of the containers to your property. For example, lead-effect planters look great with older properties, modern apartments call for more up-to-date materials, such as zinc, and cottage gardens are enhanced by informal containers, such as terracotta or stone.

My Top Tips for Choosing Containers

The bigger the container, the better (this will ensure that watering is needed less frequently and that your plants have room to grow).

Deeper pots are better than shallow ones.

Ensure containers have at least one drainage hole (three is better).

Pick containers that will create focal points.

Include containers of different heights and sizes in a scheme.

Types of Container

A visit to your local garden centre will present you with a vast array of pots, window boxes and planters in a range of sizes, colours and materials. You'll also see hanging baskets, wall baskets and plant stands. For more unusual displays, and to give your scheme a personal touch, try visiting junk shops and local sales to find objects that can be recycled and turned into containers. Look out for old sinks, metal troughs, old tins, galvanised metal buckets, tin baths, wooden wine crates and onion boxes, and wicker baskets. Don't worry if what you find doesn't have a drainage hole, as these are easy to make in metal and wooden containers (see page 32).

Container Materials

Natural materials, such as terracotta, stone and wood, make the best containers for plants, being more cooling for roots and ensuring plants don't overheat. You can also buy very good imitation terracotta and stone versions that are just as appealing visually and less expensive. Look for containers made from reconstituted stone and lighter materials such as fibre glass. Lighter containers may be the best option for a balcony or roof garden where weight is a consideration. Wood is also a great choice, but bear in mind that it can rot over time.

Painting Containers

Quite a few of the containers in this book were specially made, such as the Hanging and Ground Turquoise Planters (see page 149). I also painted lots of the containers, including the Ombré Herb Pots (see page 161) and the Succulent Trough (see page 145). Painting and spray-painting are great ways to create a unique container – you can choose just the right shade and texture to suit your planting scheme.

Preparing Containers for Painting

Always clean your container thoroughly first to create the best surface for the paint or spray paint. Run the container under water and scrub lightly with a dish-washing brush or pot bristle brush to remove all the dust and dirt. Terracotta pots can build up a crusty white residue over time, due to salts and other chemicals that are often found in tap water. This is not an ideal surface for painting, so I suggest a more thorough clean first (see page 32 for guidance on cleaning terracotta pots). Also, check that your container is completely dry before you paint it, especially terracotta pots, which readily absorb moisture. Put your containers in the sun to speed up the drying process.

You can also use a paint primer first, which lays a good foundation for the paint, gives a smoother finish and improves the paint's durability. There are primers suitable for different materials, including metal, wood, terracotta, stone and even plastic.

Painting and Spray-painting

Buying paint, especially for larger containers, can be expensive, so purchase some tester pots first to see if you like the colour and effect it creates.

You can use a wide range of exterior paints on wooden containers such as troughs, boxes and crates. Try ordinary exterior emulsion and oil-based gloss paint. For metal containers, it's best to use gloss paint or a proprietary metal paint. Terracotta pots can be painted with non-toxic acrylic or emulsion paints or spray-painted. Concrete or stone pots can also be painted with emulsion or a specialist masonry paint suitable for exteriors. There are also outdoor stains available for wooden containers. Note that these are affected by the colour of the wood you're staining. Always place your container on a dust sheet or newspaper first to protect your working surface.

Start by applying a base coat using a household paintbrush or try a foam brush for a smoother result. Apply second and even third coats, depending on the type and colour of paint you're using, as well as whether you want any of the container to show through. You don't need to paint the bottom or inside of the container, although you can paint the top inch or so that won't be covered with potting mix. Allow the container to dry thoroughly before planting up. This may take some time, especially if the container is made of terracotta. To avoid the paint chipping or cracking, you can apply a matte or gloss varnish to seal the paint (following the manufacturer's directions).

To spray-paint a container, work outdoors or in a well-ventilated space. Hold the can about 30 cm (12 in) from the surface and spray in a steady back-and-forth motion.

LOAD-BEARING
CONSIDERATIONS

If you only have a balcony or roof garden, it is essential to check with an architect or structural engineer how much weight the space can take before committing to buying containers and plants. If you are planning any major work, such as building raised beds, then also check whether planning permission is required. Make sure you find out whether the balcony is waterproof. Better safe than sorry here, as there is nothing worse than having to pay for flooding your home or your neighbour's below, or even causing the roof/balcony to collapse under the weight of heavy containers. Remember, a fully watered container is very heavy, so it's best to place containers near load-bearing walls, or over a load-bearing beam or joist.

Slowly rotate the container as you spray. Try to keep the spray can the same distance from the container to ensure an even coverage. Wait a few minutes before applying a second or third coat. Always follow the manufacturer's instructions.

Designing Container Plantings

Putting together wonderful planting displays in containers is both creative and rewarding. From a single specimen in a large planter to miniature 'borders' of flowers and foliage in a collection of containers, the opportunities for experimenting with colours, patterns and shapes are endless.

There is a useful phrase to remember when you are designing a container scheme: 'Thriller, filler and spiller'. This can be helpful when you're working out the design for a container and how to compose your plant combinations. For example, if you have a large container, you might want some tall plants at the back to provide height (the 'thriller' or focus plant) and then some shorter plants to fill up the middle area of the container (the 'filler' plants). To finish the planting, you could choose plants that trail over the sides (the 'spiller' plants). Here is a list of my favourite thrillers, fillers and spillers (which is by no means exhaustive):

Thrillers Argyranthemum, azalea, campanula, dahlia, delphinium, euphorbia, ferns, fuchsia, grasses, hydrangeas, lavenders, lupins, phormium, pittosporum, sweet peas, tall verbena, veronica

Fillers Anemone, antirrhinum, aquilegia, aster, astrantia, coleus, cosmos, diascia, heuchera, impatiens, pot marigolds, matthiola, osteospermum, poppies, pelargonium, salvia, tiarella, vinca, zinnia

Spillers Calibrachoa, erigeron, ipomoea, lobelia, petunia, trailing ivy, trailing verbena

Putting it All Together

I always have great fun deciding on colour schemes and plants for containers each year. They are a real source of joy and satisfaction for me. The plants you choose inevitably come down to taste and the location in which you're gardening, but I have put together a few pointers here that should prove helpful, especially if you're new to growing plants in containers:

Planting in odd numbers is the most aesthetically pleasing to the eye, so plant one, three or five plants in a container.

Consider restricting the colour scheme, opting for shades of one or two complementary colours. This is because too many colours can make a display look too busy and your space smaller – unless, of course, your intention is a cacophony of colour!

Remember 'Thriller, filler, spiller': choose a focal plant and complement it with a mixture of upright bedding plants and those that will trail over the sides of the container.

Use a focal plant such as evergreen box, lavender or bay to provide year-round interest to which you can ring in the seasonal changes – by underplanting with perennials and annuals for summer and bulbs for spring and autumn.

Combine plants that have similar growing requirements for the best results. For example, combine plants that prefer full sun or those that require partial or full shade.

For small-scale containers, look for dwarf varieties or alpines that will be happier in more confined conditions.

Opt for drought-resistant plants such as cacti and succulents, or perhaps sun-loving herbs, if you don't think you can commit to a daily watering regime for them.

Tip — Hardy plants, including shrubs such as lavender and herbaceous perennials like fuchsias and lupins, can be grown in containers and then eventually planted out in the open garden, or replanted in a larger pot.

Dahlia (Thriller)

Salvia (Filler)

Cosmos (Filler)

Euphorbium (Filler)

Ipomea (Spiller)

Echinacea (Thriller)

Osteospermum (Filler)

Achillea (Filler)

Ivy (Spiller)

Planting Mediums

There will be a wide selection of potting mixes on offer at your local garden centre and online. Take some time to read up about the different types that are available, as that way you will be sure of choosing the best one for each container planting. There are two main types of potting mix: soil-based potting mix and soil-less potting mix.

Soil-based Potting Mixes

A soil-based potting mix is a reliable, all-purpose mix containing a combination of sterilised loam (soil), peat, sharp sand and fertilisers, making it perfect for most containers. It provides plants with a good supply of nutrients for the weeks immediately after planting and retains moisture well. It is also free-draining, which encourages roots to grow. You will see three types of soil-based potting mix for sale in the UK (see page 175 for information about potting mixes elsewhere), made according to formulae devised by the John Innes Institute, a well-regarded plant science research centre in Norfolk, with each one being suitable for different scenarios, as follows:

For seeds and cuttings (John Innes No. 1)
This potting mix is lightweight and low in nutrients. Seedlings will need potting into larger pots as they grow.

For annuals and perennials (John Innes No. 2)
This is a slightly heavier, richer potting mix, containing more nutrients to encourage the growth of roots and foliage. You can also get bulb potting mix which contains added horticultural sand or grit to provide a free-draining planting medium suitable for growing bulbs.

For permanent plantings (John Innes No. 3)
This potting mix is high in nutrients and free-draining, and also contains slow-release fertiliser, making it ideal for trees, shrubs and bamboos that will be growing permanently in a container.

Soil-less Potting Mixes

As the name indicates, this type of potting mix doesn't contain any loam (soil). Instead, it is usually peat- or peat-substitute-based. If you are at all concerned about the environmental impact of removing peat from bogs to make peat-based potting mix, then choose one made from a peat substitute such as coir or wood fibre. These are now nearly as good as peat-based potting mixes.

Soil-less potting mixes are perfectly adequate for most types of plants. They have the advantage of being lighter than soil-based potting mixes, both to transport and in situ, plus they are also often cheaper and ideal for small containers. Their main drawback is that they tend to dry out very quickly and can be very difficult to re-hydrate once dry. For this reason, it is a good idea to add some moisture-retaining granules to the potting mix when you plant up your containers. You will also need to feed plants grown in this type of potting mix regularly to keep nutrient levels topped up. I advise against using them for long-term container plantings.

Specialist Potting Mixes

Also available are potting mixes designed for specific types of plants. Plants that require a specialist potting mix include cacti and succulents, which need extra grit for drainage. If you can't get hold of cacti and succulent potting mix, then just use a general-purpose potting mix and add some horticultural sand or grit to make it more free-draining. There are also ericaceous potting mixes with a pH lower than seven. These are lime-free and designed for acid-loving plants such as heathers, camellias, azaleas and rhododendrons.

Using Additives

Although not essential, it can be beneficial to incorporate various additives into the potting mix before planting your container. They improve drainage and make it more effective.

Horticultural sand or grit Use these additives to improve drainage – perhaps if you are growing alpines, herbs or cacti and succulents. If you are growing seedlings or very small plants, then use only sand or fine gr`avel to avoid damaging their delicate roots. Sand and grit can also be used to add weight to a potting mix, which may be helpful if you are growing a top-heavy plant.

Perlite This is a naturally occurring white volcanic glass that helps to aerate the potting mix and improve drainage. It is lightweight too, making it useful in containers for balconies and roof gardens where weight is a consideration. Also ideal for hanging baskets.

Vermiculite An expanded mineral, this additive is usually grey or beige in colour. Use it for the same purposes as perlite.

Water-retaining gel With watering being the key to successful container gardening, adding some water-retaining gel is a great idea. The granular material swells up when wet, providing the plants with water so you do not have to water them as often. I recommend adding this to the potting mix when planting summer containers and hanging baskets.

PREPARATION AND PLANTING

Preparing Your Containers

Cleaning your containers before planting them up reduces the risk of pests and diseases infecting your precious new plants. Scrub the container with some warm soapy water and rinse thoroughly, then allow to dry.

Cleaning Terracotta Pots

Terracotta pots can start looking very dirty and crusty. Although some people like this aged effect, it's worth pointing out that using dirty pots again and again without cleaning them is not great for your plants. To be honest, if a terracotta pot is looking crusty, the plant has probably been growing in it for too long and should be repotted in fresh potting mix.

1. Use a dish-washing brush or pot bristle brush to clean as much dirt and old potting mix from the inside and outside of the pot.

2. Soak the pot in a solution of water and white vinegar. You'll need about 250 ml (8 fl oz/1 cup) of vinegar to every 750 ml or 1 litre (25 or 34 fl oz/ 3 or 4 cups) of water. Obviously, the stronger the vinegar concentration, the less time you'll need to soak the pot. Submerge the pot in the solution. The vinegar will start working on the crusty build-up. After about 20–30 minutes, see if you can wipe or scrub off the residue. Leave for longer, if necessary, and use the brush to scrub firmly to remove the residue.

3. Finally, put the pot in the dishwasher on the quick wash cycle. This will clean and disinfect the pot ready for planting. Alternatively, scrub the pots in warm soapy water and rinse well.

Check for Drainage Holes

It is important to ensure that all containers have a drainage hole or holes in the bottom. Most plants dislike sitting in very wet soil, so excess water needs to be able to drain out of the container to prevent the potting mix becoming waterlogged. Although most containers already have drainage holes, recycled items such as metal buckets or wooden crates probably won't. However, it is easy to make holes in these with a hammer and heavy-duty nail. Just turn the container over and hit the nail hard with the hammer to make a series of holes in the bottom. You can also use an electric drill to make the holes. Obviously, containers made from stone, terracotta or ceramics cannot be treated in this way, in which case use them for indoor plants or, if you keep them outdoors, water carefully and keep checking that the potting mix isn't becoming too waterlogged.

Adding Drainage Crocks

Water needs to be able to drain freely from the bottom of your containers, so it's a good idea to cover the drainage holes with a few pieces of broken terracotta pot, old tiles, or old china (often referred to as 'crocks'). This will prevent the drainage holes clogging up with potting mix. To make crocks, put the broken pots, tiles, etc. in a plastic bag – so that flying pieces don't hit you – then smash them with a hammer. You might want to wear sunglasses or protective goggles when doing this. Aim for pieces that are about 3–4 cm (1–1½ in) square. You then simply add a few handfuls of drainage crocks to the bottom of the container before planting.

I suggest collecting a stash of crocks, perhaps in an old pot, so you always have some to hand ready for new containers. You can also use pieces of polystyrene as drainage material (which is ideal for keeping the weight down on roof gardens and balconies).

Giving Your Plants a Good Soak

To give your plants the best possible start, I advise soaking their root balls in water before planting. Simply immerse the root ball in a large bucket of water for 10–20 minutes. The time this takes will depend on the size of your plant. Look for when air bubbles stop bursting out of the surface of the potting mix, as this is a sign that it is soaked through.

Loosening Plant Roots

When you take a plant out of its plastic growing pot, the roots may look pot-bound. Before planting it up in a new container, use your fingers to gently tease out the roots to loosen them and encourage them to spread out and grow in their new home. Try not to damage the root system when you do this.

HOW TO LINE WOODEN OR WICKER CONTAINERS

If the container (or window box) is made from wood or wicker, make sure it is lined with black plastic sheeting before planting (to prevent rotting). Alternatively, you can use a plastic inner container and fill around this with potting mix.

1. Cut a piece of sheeting that's large enough to line the container.

2. Drape the sheeting in the container and tuck it neatly into the corners.

3. Use a staple gun to fix the sheeting in place just below the rim of the container.

4. Make sure you cut a few holes in the sheeting to allow for drainage. Then plant up your container as usual.

Planting Techniques

Whether you're potting up a single specimen or a selection of different plants, the technique for planting a container is identical. The techniques for hanging baskets and window boxes are slightly different.

Planting Pots and Planters

If you have bought a new container, you can start planting without any preparation. However, if you are reusing old containers, then I advise washing these thoroughly in case fungal or other diseases, or sometimes the eggs of certain pests, are lurking in the residues of old potting mix (see page 50–51).

1. Soak the plant (or plants) for about 10–20 minutes, depending on their size. This consolidates the potting mix around the root ball, which makes the plant easier to handle. Allow to drain.

2. Cover the hole in the bottom of the container (there may be more than one) with a few drainage crocks. This improves drainage and prevents the potting mix being washed out of the container when you water.

3. If you wish, you can also add a few scoops of gravel to the bottom of the container to improve drainage.

4. Although not essential, adding some vermiculite (see page 29) to the potting mix can also help to improve drainage.

5. Add a few scoops of potting mix to the bottom of the container. I like to use a special container potting mix that already has a good supply of fertiliser and water-storing granules.

6. Mix the vermiculite (if using) into the layer of potting mix with your fingers.

7. Fill the container with potting mix until it is about two-thirds full and firm down gently with your hands.

8. Tease out the roots of the plant gently with your fingers. Sit the plant in the container to check the planting depth. Once the container is planted up, the surface of the potting mix should be an inch or so below the rim to allow for watering. Add or remove potting mix to adjust the level, as required. If you are using more than one plant, arrange the other plants around the first, ensuring all the root balls are level.

9. Add scoops of potting mix to fill the gap between the plant and the sides of the container, or between the selection of plants.

10. Firm in gently and level off. Be careful not to press too firmly because this can compact the surface of the potting mix and stop water draining.

11. Once the potting mix has settled, check whether you need to add more potting mix to create a level surface. If you wish, you can add a layer of fine gravel or other decorative trim. This adds a nice finishing touch, while also providing a mulch that slows down the evaporation of water from the container.

12. Position the container then water well, ideally using a watering can fitted with a fine rose attachment. Allow it to drain.

Tip — From experience, I have found it's best to plant containers in the early morning or late afternoon, when it's a little cooler. I always make sure the plants have plenty of water when they are planted along with some plant fertiliser.

Planting Window Boxes and Troughs

Window boxes are ideal if you don't have a garden – they can be used on balconies and roof gardens – and add instant kerb appeal to any property. Remember that window boxes on the upper levels of a building need to be properly secured to avoid accidents. Also bear in mind that a window box will be heavy, especially when filled with potting mix and watered.

1. Plant a window box in the same way as a container, but remember that it is usually only seen from one side. Imagine that the box is a tiny garden border, or even a theatre stage, and arrange the plants accordingly.

2. Start with the larger plants towards the back and add smaller plants at the front. Trailing plants such as ivy can be used to cascade over the edges and soften the effect. Repeating plants in the box can also be useful for creating a sense of unity.

How to Make a Hanging Planter

(see *Hanging and Ground Turquoise Planters* p. 149)

1. Drill 4 holes in either corner of the planter.

2. Take 4 lengths of chain with a key ring secured on each end and feed through so the key ring is secured underneath the rim of the planter.

3. Take 2 lengths at one end and secure with another key ring so you can hang the planter.

4. Repeat on the other end.

2 (Hanging planter steps)

3 (Hanging planter steps)

SECURING A WINDOW BOX

It is vital that the window box is fixed securely in place. Either add two nails or hook eyes on either side and attach pieces of wire to stop the window box falling, or use special window box brackets to screw it to a window sill, wall or railings. You can get adjustable brackets that can take different weights: small brackets can support 20 kg (44 lb) and large brackets 40 kg (80 lb). Balcony hooks, for both normal and wider balcony ledges, are also available.

Planting Hanging Baskets

Perfect for providing a splash of colour throughout the summer, hanging baskets are usually flamboyant and filled with flowers, many of which cascade over the edge and trail down.

1. Place your containers on a clean, flat surface.

2. Start by lining the basket with moss or a hanging basket liner.

3. If you are using moss, you'll need to use some black plastic sheeting or other suitable liner to retain the potting mix. Use scissors to cut a large circle that will fit inside the moss lining. Cut a few small holes or slits in the plastic or liner at the base for drainage.

4. Cut a few small holes or slits in the plastic or liner at the base for drainage. Fill the basket about one-third full with potting mix, then firm in gently with your fingers.

5. Start by planting the sides of the basket. Make slits in the moss/liner and push through the root balls of the plants so they are resting on the surface of the potting mix. Cover the root balls of the plants with more potting mix.

6. Next, plant the top of the basket. It is advisable to have one main plant in the middle and then add smaller, trailing plants around the edge.

7. Suspend the hanging basket using S-hooks and metal chains.

Creating a Suspended Sphere

Prepare the lower half of the sphere as you would a conventional hanging basket, then use galvanised metal wire to secure a second basket to the first to create a striking plant sphere. If you wish, you can spray-paint the hanging baskets first. See Suspended Spheres, on page 69, for advice on fixing the together and suspending the sphere.

Tips — Place the unplanted basket on the rim of a bucket or old container to make planting easier.

Use a lightweight potting mix in baskets because they will be heavy once planted and watered.

As hanging baskets are usually less accessible than conventional containers, add some all-purpose fertiliser granules to the potting mix before planting up.

1

2

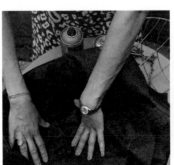
3

4

Finishing Touches

Although not essential by any means, you can add a few finishing touches to your planted containers and their surroundings to lift them out of the ordinary and make them more stylish and eye-catching.

Decorative Trims

One of the easiest ways to enhance a container is by adding a decorative trim. There is a huge selection available in garden centres and online. Not only do these look more attractive than bare potting mix but they also serve a practical purpose – they help cut down weeds and also reduce the rate of water evaporation from the potting mix. Try to match the choice of trim to the style of the container and the planting.

Cotswold chippings   Usually creamy white or beige, Cotswold chippings make a crisp, clean and stylish trim for containers.

Gravel/grit   Available in a wealth of colours, gravel is ideal for many different plants.

Moss   Both sheet and cushion moss, available from florists and garden centres, produce a lovely, natural trim for most plant displays.

Pebbles   Beautiful pebbles, large or small, enhance many planting schemes, especially those associated with seashore plants like sea holly and thrift. Please note: don't be tempted to remove pebbles and shells from beaches.

Slate   Always stylish, grey slate looks especially good with plants grown in metal containers, whether these are window boxes or large dolly tubs.

Lighting   Strip lighting can be attached with silicon to edges and is an easy way to add lighting to floors and steps.

Cushions   Outdoor cushions and rugs are a great way to personalise your outdoor living area.

Floors   Mosaic tiles add charm to outdoor spaces – the tiles opposite are from Bert & May, who produce some great geometric designs.

Turf   Although I prefer natural grass, astroturf makes outside spaces such as balconies and roof terraces much more lush and can be used to cover up unsightly flooring.

Ornaments   Glass sculptures and garden ornaments make your outdoor displays unique.

Displaying Containers

You can make a real feature of your collection by displaying it on a plant stand. They often have shelves, which means you can display more than one container if space is limited. Even a simple A-frame ladder can be turned into a plant stand. Bear in mind that the plants on lower shelves may receive less light, so position your plants accordingly.

Tips — Over time the various chemicals in decorative trims will leach into the potting mix when you water the container. To avoid this when growing a single specimen, you can use a piece of horticultural fleece or membrane cut to the same diameter as the container. Cut a slit through to the middle and a small hole to accommodate the stem of the plant. Then place this on the surface of the potting mix before you add the trim. The fleece/membrane is permeable and so will let water percolate through to the plant.

Water containers on plant stands and *étagères* individually to ensure that each plant is watered properly. This is much better than watering from the top and hoping the water will trickle into all the containers below.

CARING FOR CONTAINER PLANTS

Watering and Feeding

Unlike plants grown in the open garden, container-grown plants rely on you to provide a regular supply of water and food to meet their needs. Rain often fails to reach plants growing in containers and the nutrients in the potting mix will eventually be depleted after planting.

Watering

You will need to water your container plants more frequently when they are in active growth, usually in the spring and summer. Check moisture levels daily from mid-spring to early autumn – if possible, do this twice a day in hot weather. The best way to do this is by sticking your finger in the container to a depth of about 10 cm (4 in) to feel how dry the potting mix is. You can also buy a special gauge to read the moisture level.

When to Water

In summer, water early in the morning and again, if necessary, in the cool of the evening. Don't water containers during the hottest part of the day. In winter, water in late morning whenever you think the plants are in need of a drink. Water will seldom be necessary in winter for deciduous or other dormant plants, although conifers and other evergreens may benefit from a little winter water.

How Often to Water

Bedding plants in containers will require watering every day, especially in the summer. Succulents and drought-tolerant plants like herbs will need less water. Mature and well-established plants can also survive longer without water than newly planted specimens. You need to water even if it has rained, as the foliage of the plants creates an 'umbrella' that stops the rainwater reaching the potting mix.

How to Water

The best way to water is to move from container to container with a gently running garden hose aimed at the potting mix. You can also use a watering can with a fine rose attachment. Although more time-consuming, this is better for plants with delicate flowers and leaves. Water the containers thoroughly, filling them to the brim and allowing the water to drain out. Fill the containers for a second time to ensure the potting mix is thoroughly wet. If you don't see water draining out of the container, check to see if the drainage holes are blocked. Aim for slow, steady watering to give the potting mix enough time absorb the water.

If you find watering a real chore, then you can install automatic watering systems that will drip water into your containers at set times. This might be helpful if you are going on holiday. You can also get adjustable water reservoirs that turn ordinary containers into self-watering planters. However, you will still need to pay close attention to the watering requirements of your plants and respond accordingly.

Under- and Over-watering

It can be easy to give plants too little or too much water. Signs that your plants are being under-watered include dropping petals, dry, shrivelled and discoloured leaves, and limp stems. You might also notice a whitish bloom on the foliage. If the potting mix has dried out completely, try rehydrating it and reviving the plant (see opposite).

Over-watering is a common mistake. Aim to keep potting mix moist but not soggy as plants don't like sitting in wet conditions. Avoid letting the potting mix dry out completely, then saturating it.

Signs that you are over-watering include water-soaked spots on the leaves that develop into raised swellings or growths. These can burst and look white and powdery or rust-coloured and scaly. Don't be tempted to remove the affected leaves, as this can make things worse. Instead, check whether the potting mix is free-draining (the drainage hole may be blocked, for example) – if it is too wet, it's a good idea to repot the plant using fresh potting mix.

Watering Cacti and Succulents

If you grow these plants, perhaps for the Succulent Trough (see page 145), use the soak-and-dry-out method: allow the potting mix to almost dry out before watering the plants again.

REJUVENATING A CONTAINER-GROWN PLANT

Even the most experienced gardener will have discovered a plant wilting sadly in potting mix that has completely dried out. To revive the plant, try moving the container to a cool, shady area. Soak the plant carefully on a regular basis and gently spray the leaves, and cut back any shrivelled foliage. You can also try plunging the container in a large bucket of water for about 30 minutes until the potting mix is soaked and the leaves starting to plump up again, then remove the container and allow to drain. Wait a few weeks before throwing the plant away, as you might find that it starts to sprout again – and all is not lost.

Tip — In hot weather, group containers together in a shady spot to create a microclimate that will keep the air around the foliage humid and the plants cool. This will reduce the heat stress experienced by the plants.

Feeding

Container-grown plants usually have enough nutrients in the potting mix after planting to last about six weeks. You'll then need to feed them regularly during the growing season – usually from mid-spring to early autumn – to encourage lots of flowers and strong growth. You can use a general-purpose fertiliser, which contains sufficient amounts of the three main chemicals required by plants: nitrogen, phosphorous and potassium (NPK). Nitrogen is important for healthy green leaves; phosphorus encourages root growth; and potassium promotes flowers and fruit. Ensure the feed you use contains lots of potassium for bedding plants to encourage lots of flowers – tomato fertiliser contains a good amount of potassium, so use this diluted on summer annuals. There are different types of fertiliser, as follows:

Liquid Feeds and Soluble Powders or Granules

You can buy these for general-purpose use or for specific plant types, including tomatoes, roses and strawberries. Simply use water to dilute or dissolve the fertiliser in a watering can according to the manufacturer's instructions and apply every seven to 14 days throughout the growing season.

Slow-release Fertiliser Granules

If you are short of time, or likely to lose track of a feeding routine, then try using fertiliser granules. You can either add them to the potting mix when you plant a new container or work them into the top layer of potting mix for existing containers. The nutrients are then slowly released over a period of time as you water your plants. Continuous release plant food is also available that only requires one application for the entire growing season. Follow the manufacturer's directions carefully because the dose varies depending on the plants and situation.

Foliar Feeds

Designed to give plants a quick nutrient boost, diluted foliar feeds are sprayed onto the plants rather than being added to the potting mix. Spray the undersides of the leaves as well for maximum absorption. Avoid spraying the plants in bright sunlight because this can lead to sun-scorch as the solution dries.

Top-dressing

If you have plants growing permanently in containers – usually mature shrubs like pittosporum or phormiums – they can be top-dressed to keep them healthy and thriving. Use your fingers to remove as much of the potting mix as possible from the top of the container. Then add fresh potting mix (with some added fertiliser if you wish) and water thoroughly. Firm down well to eliminate any air pockets.

Tips — Bear in mind that plants such as herbs, cacti and succulents, and wild flowers, prefer poorer soils and so need fewer added nutrients. For these plants, I suggest using half the recommended dose of general-purpose fertiliser.

You can buy specialist fertilisers for ericaceous plants, roses, and cacti and succulents.

If you are using soil-less potting mix, check that any fertiliser you apply contains essential trace elements, such as iron, manganese, zinc and copper.

Calendar of Care

Container gardening is ideal if you are low on time and space, because you only have a small area to look after. Seasonal tasks in the container garden are a lovely way to mark the various stages of the horticultural year.

Spring

Begin a winter tidy, checking containers for frost damage and giving them a good clean ready for planting.

Remove any dead, diseased or damaged growth from overwintering plants (see page 49).

Gradually remove winter protection such as horticultural fleece from tender specimens like cycads, tree ferns and bananas.

Give all existing containers a thorough first watering – even if it is raining outside. Water containers several times and check that water has run freely out of the drainage holes.

Continue watering and begin feeding container-grown plants regularly.

Plant bulbs such as dahlias, alliums and lilies that will flower in summer.

Visit garden centres and nurseries (or shop online) to buy new bedding plants. If you shop online, you may have to wait a few weeks for the plants to arrive.

Start planting new containers when all danger of frosts has passed.

Repot any plants that have outgrown their container.

Check whether permanent plantings – of shrubs and bamboos, for example – need potting into a larger pot, or top-dress with fresh potting mix if they are too large to move.

Lift and divide any perennials whose growth is looking woody.

In early spring, clip topiary plants such as box for the first time in the year.

Remember to label new seeds, plants or bulbs.

Protect new plants from slugs.

Summer

Keep planting new containers with summer flowers – garden centres and nurseries will have a good choice on offer.

Maintain a regular watering and feeding routine. Remember to water your plants daily (twice daily, if possible) during hot spells. Feed every seven to 14 days.

If you are going on holiday, ensure a friend or neighbour can continue watering and feeding while you are away. If not, move all containers together to a shady spot.

Deadhead flowering annuals and tender perennials to promote further flushes of flowers.

Stake any tall-growing plants that may benefit from some support.

Check every day for pests and diseases – then act quickly as soon as you spot any signs of trouble.

Cut back the leaves of spring-flowering bulbs when they turn yellow.

Lightly prune or cut back early-flowering perennials such as campanulas.

Continue clipping topiary plants and give them their last clip of the year in late summer.

Snip sprigs regularly from herbs like rosemary to keep the plants nice and bushy.

Autumn

Empty and clean containers used for summer bedding plants. Dispose of the plants.

Remove dahlias from their pots and dry off the tubers. Store the tubers in a cool, dry place for planting out again next year.

Remove dead flowers and foliage from permanent plantings. Also remove fallen leaves from the tops of containers.

Prune and cut back any dead, diseased or damaged stems from trees and shrubs.

Divide spring-flowering perennials such as hostas.

Overwinter suitable perennials (see page 49).

Plant new containers with spring-flowering bulbs – they will be something to look forward to over the winter.

Winter

If very cold weather is forecast, protect container plants at night, moving them to a sheltered spot, such as near a house wall or under cover. This will prevent the roots freezing.

Although most plants are dormant at this time of year, check whether any plants, especially evergreens, are showing signs of flagging and water accordingly.

Visit garden centres and nurseries to buy plants such as cyclamen, winter pansies and heathers for planting up containers for winter interest.

Plan and design container schemes for next year, ordering plant catalogues and looking online for inspiration.

Keeping Plants Neat and Tidy

Plants grown in containers need as much care and attention as those grown in the open garden. Pruning and deadheading are the most important tasks to keep your plants looking their best.

Pruning

Pruning is used to control the size of the plant, and usually involves lightly clipping permanent plantings of established evergreen shrubs such as box and bay. The best time to prune plants such as these is in spring and summer. You can use topiary shears to trim soft young growth, but you will need a pair of secateurs to tackle tougher stems. Also remove any dead, diseased or damaged growth when you spot it to keep your plants both tidy and healthy.

Deadheading

This is the removal of dead or fading blooms from plants to encourage them to produce a further flush of flowers, instead of using their energy to produce seeds. It also keeps them looking attractive. Simply pinch off spent flowers or remove them with a pair of scissors. Most bedding plants, including pelargoniums and petunias, respond well to deadheading, as do herbaceous perennials such as heuchera, lupins, cosmos, diascia and dahlias.

Tidying Grasses

Grasses bring a feathery touch to container schemes, but you'll find that dead material tends to build up. This prevents new leaves from growing well and also looks untidy. Simply run your fingers through the grass to pull out old leaves. If the grass has tough or sharp leaves, protect your hands by wearing gardening gloves. Some older growth may need to be tackled with a pair of scissors or in some instances secateurs.

Staking

This is usually unnecessary for plants grown in containers, especially if you are planting dwarf varieties of species, but taller plants such as delphiniums, dahlias, lupins and achilleas can benefit from some form of support to stop the stems bending over or even snapping. I like to use garden ties attached to garden canes, which you can paint green so they are less obtrusive, but you can also use string or raffia.

Overwintering Plants

Most container plants are fleeting annuals and tender perennials that are thrown away at the end of summer. However, you can overwinter some perennials, along with trees and shrubs growing permanently in containers, to enjoy for another year.

Overwintering Perennials

Some gardeners get rid of container perennials once the season is over, while others like to plant them out in the garden and start with new perennials the following year. To survive cold winter temperatures and winds, however, container-grown plants need a little extra attention. This is because their roots are above ground and are therefore susceptible to frost; if the roots freeze, then this can result in the death of the plant.

Container plants can also be temporarily moved closer to house walls to get them through a very cold spell. Similarly, in very wet weather, moving containers under cover to allow soaking potting mix to dry out a little can help avoid frost damage – again, the rain shadow created by a wall is fine. You can also overwinter container plants in an unheated greenhouse or porch if you have one. Alternatively, just put the container in a slightly larger pot to create an extra layer of insulation around the roots.

Keeping Bulbs for Next Year

Plants such as daffodils and grape hyacinths have underground storage bulbs, which means they can be kept from year to year. To keep bulbs in containers, remove the flowers as they fade to stop the plant setting seed. Water and feed the plant as the leaves yellow and die back to give the plant a boost so that it will produce good flowers the following year. You can also remove dahlia tubers from their pots and dry them off. Store the tubers in a cool, dry place ready for planting out again next year.

SOME PERENNIALS THAT OVERWINTER WELL

This list is by no means exhaustive, but it includes reliable perennials that can be overwintered in containers for the following year.

Yarrow	X Heucherella
Bellflower	Salvia (perennials only)
Coneflower	Stonecrop
Ferns	Houseleeks
Coral flower	Hens and chicks
Hosta	Foamflower

Dealing with Pests, Diseases and Disorders

Checking regularly for pests and diseases is the best line of defence for keeping plants healthy and looking good. If you don't tackle problems quickly, pests and diseases can easily ruin your displays. Here I look at the most common problems that affect container plants and suggest ways to tackle them. Where possible, I advise using physical remedies before resorting to chemical solutions such as insecticides, pesticides and fungicides. If you're uncertain about identifying pests and diseases, look for images online to help you.

Common Pests

Aphids (Greenfly and Blackfly)

Most people are familiar with aphids, which are usually first spotted in the spring sucking on plant sap. They infest the tips of shoots, flower buds and the undersides of leaves. Their feeding can cause distorted growth. Aphids also carry viruses in their mouthparts that can cause further problems, including stunted growth.

What to do? As soon as you see signs of aphid infestation, spray the aphids off with a garden hose. An organic solution is to look for ladybirds, the natural predators of aphids, and place them on the affected plant so they can control the pests for you. Encouraging other predators such as lacewings and hoverflies (the larvae eat the aphids) can also be beneficial. Try planting yarrow, cosmos, marigold, fennel and lemon balm to attract them. You can spray with a commercial organic insecticide if you wish or, alternatively, with a diluted solution of water and washing-up liquid.

Slugs and Snails

Perhaps the gardener's most irritating enemy, slugs and snails quickly devour young plant growth. Growing plants in containers does not provide protection. Slugs and snails are night-time feeders, and tell-tale signs that they are visiting are unsightly holes in the leaves of plants as well as their slimy trails.

What to do? Try to avoid using slug pellets and other poisons, and tackle slugs by hand. This is relatively easy with a container garden. Get into the habit of checking your containers in the evening and after it has rained, and picking the slugs off. Remember to look underneath containers as they often hide there. You can also use lengths of copper tape around the rims of containers – this gives slugs an electric shock when it reacts with their mucus.

Vine Weevil

Container plants are vulnerable to this pest. Adult weevils eat the edges of leaves in summer, but it is the white, legless larvae that cause the most damage. The adults are most active from spring to late summer, with the females laying their eggs in the potting mix. The emerging larvae then overwinter in the container, feasting from autumn to spring on roots and often causing the plant to wilt or even die. You may not notice that your plants have been under attack until spring if you pot the plants on.

What to do? Inspect plants in the evening in spring and summer to find adult weevils. The most effective control is to kill the grubs as they emerge, so look out for damage to leaves by the adults and then introduce a parasitic nematode to the potting mix. Parasitic nematodes are microscopic organisms that are watered into the potting mix. They feed on the pests and also breed. You may need a few applications to ensure success. Systemic insecticides for vine weevils are also available if you are happy to use chemicals.

Common Diseases

Botrytis (Grey Mould)

This fluffy grey mould is very common, particularly in wet and poorly ventilated conditions. The disease is easily passed from one plant to another.

What to do? Spray with an organic fungicide after cutting back all affected growth. To reduce the chances of contamination, ensure plants in neighbouring containers aren't touching each other. You may also want to prune out congested stems.

Leaf Spots

You may see coloured spots on the leaves of plants in spring and summer – usually brown, black or yellow. These are caused by various fungi. The problem is exacerbated by damp weather.

What to do? Remove affected leaves, then spray the plant with an organic fungicide. The plant will need a nutrient boost after this, so apply a liquid or foliar feed.

Powdery Mildew

A dry white powder coating leaves, shoot tips and occasionally flowers is a sign of this disease. Plants may also become stunted and flower less reliably. Inadequate watering may be the cause.

What to do? Make sure there is sufficient air flow around plants and that the growing conditions are suitable. Remove infected parts. Ensure they are well watered.

Root Rot

If plants suddenly wilt and die, this can be a result of soil-borne fungi.

What to do? Use fresh potting mix and ensure containers are draining properly when they are watered. Unfortunately, it can be difficult for plants to recover from root rot once it has taken hold.

Physiological Disorders

Many plant problems aren't caused by specific pests and diseases but by difficult conditions, such as cold weather, sudden changes in temperature, or over- or underwatering. You may find that these can make leaves discolour and drop, rendering plants more vulnerable to disease. The best solution is to care for your plants as well as you can, paying close attention to watering and feeding, and ensuring they are protected from extreme cold, heat and wet, for example.

PREVENTION IS BETTER THAN CURE

Here are some tips for keeping your plants healthy and so avoiding problems in the first place:

Before buying at a garden centre or nursery, check plants carefully, looking for healthy leaves and root ball. If possible, remove the plant from its pot to check before you buy.

Look out for disease-resistant cultivars where possible.

Take the time to clean containers thoroughly before planting.

Use a good-quality potting mix to give your plants the best possible start.

Water and feed your plants regularly – like us, a healthy plant will be less susceptible to ailments as a result.

Maintain good hygiene, removing dead, diseased or dying foliage whenever you see it – perhaps when watering or deadheading. Also, regularly sweep and clear your paving, balcony or roof garden, as accumulating leaves can harbour pests and diseases. If possible, hose down the area as well.

Once planted, be sure to check your plants regularly for signs of pests and diseases. Remember to check the undersides of leaves, too.

THE
PROJECTS

Plant Care Symbols

Difficulty level

Rated from one to three, these leaves indicate how much effort and/or skill will be required to create each project, one being easy work for the beginner gardener, three being a project that will take a little more time and effort.

Seasons

These icons indicate the best planting season, or seasons, for the container. From left to right: summer, autumn, winter, spring.

Sun and shade

This illustrates where the planter should be placed in your space. From left to right: sunny, partial shade, full shade.

Edible

If any of the plants in the container are edible, such as herbs, you'll see this icon on the page.

Watering

Look for this symbol to see how much water your container will need. From left to right, one for light watering, two for moderate, three for heavy watering. Check the labels on your plants for more detailed information on frequency.

Feeding

Where you see this symbol, read the instructions here to discover how frequently your container will need feeding.

One-day project

RUSTED TONES

Medium gardening

Spring to summer

Full sun or partial shade

Moderate watering

*Feed every few weeks
in the growing season
with a general-purpose
fertiliser*

I just love the moody and beautiful combination of such delicate
pinks and dark reds with the industrial feel of the copper and
zinc pots. To my mind, this really brings a planting scheme up to
date – it would look rather tame in other planters. Alternatively,
a terracotta pot would work well here. Combining containers
and plants that have the same hues creates a more sophisticated
display suitable for many styles of garden. The focal point of this
display is undoubtedly the 'Platt's Black' New Zealand flax with
its sword-like leaves in a striking shade of purple-black. During
hot summers, this architectural show-stopper may throw up
a spike of orange flowers, which is followed by seed-heads
later in the year. Coupled with some delicate, frothy-flowered
heucherella, this statuesque plant will maintain the interest
of the display once the spring tulips and hyacinths have faded
away. Pinpoints of colour are also provided by the red stocks
and beautifully formed ranunculus. All-in-all, this is a very
grown-up display that will enhance any outdoor space.

Get the Look

What You Need

Large galvanised metal planter, about 70 cm (28 in) in diameter

Rusted metal planter, about 60 cm (24 in) in diameter

2 terracotta pots (for the smaller plants)

Electric drill or hammer and heavy-duty nail (optional)

Drainage crocks

Potting mix

Perlite or vermiculite (to improve drainage)

Metal plant stand (optional)

Plants

For the Galvanised Metal Planter

1 'Platt's Black' New Zealand flax (*Phormium*)

2 'Art Deco' heucherella (*Heucherella*)

2 'Pink Skyrocket' foam flower (*Tiarella*)

For the Rusted Metal Planter

3 'Sweet Invitation' hyacinth (*Hyacinthus*)

2 Brompton stock (*Matthiola incana*)

1 'Ranokel' ranunculus (*Ranunculus*)

2 'Apricot Beauty' tulip (*Tulipa*)

For the Terracotta Pots

1 wood sorrel in the freestanding pot (*Oxalis triangularis*)

1 'Pink Skyrocket' foam flower in the plant stand (*Tiarella*)

1. The two main planters are large, which means they will be very heavy once filled with potting mix and watered in. So, I suggest positioning them first before planting. Start with the larger metal planter, covering the hole in the bottom with a few drainage crocks to prevent it becoming blocked with potting mix. If necessary, use an electric drill or hammer and heavy-duty nail to put a hole in the bottom of the planter, as I have (see page 34).

2. Fill the planter two-thirds full with potting mix, incorporating some perlite or vermiculite to improve drainage, and position the New Zealand flax towards the back. Adjust the level of the potting mix so the top of the root ball is just below the rim of the planter.

3. Plant the heucherella and foam flower next, positioning them in front of the New Zealand flax and making sure the root balls of all three plants are level. You may have to add more underneath to raise them up. Add handfuls of potting mix around the plants to fill in any gaps, then firm in gently.

4. Repeat the planting procedure for the metal planter, but this time arrange all the plants first before filling in with potting mix to check you're happy with the display. I positioned the taller hyacinths and stocks slightly towards the back and popped the ranunculus at the front.

5. Lastly, plant up the two terracotta pots. The beauty of these smaller pots is that they can be easily moved to change the display. Water all the containers and allow to drain.

Aftercare — Remove any dead or damaged leaves from the New Zealand flax in late spring to ensure the display looks its best. The leaves of heucherella can fade and shrivel, so remove these as and when you see them to keep the display looking pristine.

Medium gardening

Late spring to summer

Full sun

Moderate watering

*Feed every two weeks
in the growing season
with a general-purpose
fertiliser*

SUMMER BRIGHTS

The simple flowers of anemones, poppies and petunias create an informal combination that is perfect for this gently curved dolly tub. The aim here is to create a kaleidoscope of colour, which is something I normally wouldn't do, but I think it is really effective here due to the flowers used. These include bright red snapdragons and cerise-pink dahlias, but feel free to experiment with your choice of plants. De Caen Group has particularly vibrant flowers that appear in late spring and puts on a dazzling show. Like the cultivars of Icelandic poppy, also included in the tub, it prefers moist, but well-drained soil. For this reason, I like to add a few handfuls of gravel along with the crocks to improve the drainage (see page 34). Poppies are charming plants that always remind me of long summer days. The annual Icelandic poppy is a little shorter than some of its larger cousins, but these early, free-flowering plants reliably produce lots of flowers in full sun or partial shade. I also included Tumbelina Susanna, a beautiful blue double-flowered trailing petunia that will cascade down the sides of the tub through the summer.

Get the Look

What You Need

Galvanised metal dolly
tub, about 90-120 cm
(35-47 in) tall and
60 cm (24 in) in diameter

Drainage crocks

Gravel, horticultural sand,
perlite or vermiculite
(to improve drainage)

Potting mix

Plants

1 'Cornish Mist' bellflower
(Campanula persicifolia)

1 red snapdragon
(Antirrhinum)

1 Da Caen Group garden
anemone (Anenome coronaria)

1 'St Brigid Lord
Lieutenant' garden
anemone (Anenome)

1 'Pink Blush' dahlia
(Dahlia)

1 'Rachel's Place' dahlia
(Dahlia)

1 Gartenzwerg Group
Icelandic poppy
(Papaver nudicaule)

1 Spring Fever Series
Icelandic poppy
(Papaver nudicaule)

1 Tumbelina Susanna
petunia (Petunia)

1. Move the tub to its final position before planting, as it will be very heavy when filled with potting mix and watered in.

2. Cover the base of the tub with a few drainage crocks, then fill with potting mix until it is about two-thirds full. Mix in a few handfuls of your chosen additive to improve the drainage (see page 34). This is an informal display, so you can position the plants where you wish, but I suggest planting the tall central bellflower first. Ensure the top of the plant's root ball is an inch or so below the rim of the tub and add or remove potting mix, as required.

3. As the tub will be viewed from all sides, surround the bellflower with the other plants, placing the smaller ones near the edge so they won't be hidden from view. Plant the petunia right at the edge so it will trail over the side.

4. Check the root balls of all the plants are level and ensure there are no gaps that could be plugged by a small plant.

5. Fill in the gaps between the plants with more potting mix and firm in gently. Water well and allow to drain.

Aftercare — Deadhead the petunia, snapdragon and dahlias regularly to encourage the plants to produce more flowers and so extend the season of interest.

Tip — You may not want to spoil your display, but the flowers of the annual Icelandic poppy can be cut for a vase indoors – simply sear the ends of the cut stems with boiling water after cutting.

Summer Brights

SPRING PLANTERS

Medium gardening

Late spring to summer

Full sun or partial shade

Moderate to heavy watering

Feed every few weeks in the growing season with a general-purpose fertiliser

If you only have a small courtyard or area of decking, or simply some space outside the back door, a collection of planters can be used to create the impression of a small garden. Here, I've chosen planters made from three different materials, but they're in similar tones so they complement each other to create an informal scheme. Although this display is at its peak in late spring and early summer, the mophead hydrangeas will continue flowering late into summer.

Hydrangeas make ideal container plants, thriving in partial shade and giving you a big, showy display of long-lasting flowers. The faded flowerheads can look beautiful in the autumn and winter, rather like faded floral fabric. Bear in mind, however, that hydrangeas need to be kept well-watered; otherwise you will have a rather wilted display. The pretty blue veronica flowers will also flower well into late summer, so extending the display's season of interest. You can refill with other annuals when the blooms have faded.

Get the Look

What You Need

Large wicker planter (such as an old log basket), about 60-90 cm (24-35 in) in diameter

Plastic planter with drainage holes (to fit inside the wicker planter)

Stone urn or similar planter, about 60 cm (24 in) in diameter

Tall grey planter, about 40-60 cm (16-24 in) in diameter

Electric drill or hammer and heavy-duty nail (optional)

Drainage crocks

Potting mix

Perlite or vermiculite (to improve drainage)

Plants

For the Wicker Planter (Red and Pink Flowers)

1 'Wine and Roses' rhododendron *(Rhododendron)*

1 'Pink and Purple' columbine *(Aquilegia Vulgaris* var. *Stellata)*

1 saxifrage *(Saxifraga)*

For the Stone Urn (White Flowers)

1 hellebore *(Helleborus)*

1 mophead hydrangea *(Hydrangea macrophylla)*

1 saxifrage *(Saxifraga)*

For the Tall Grey Planter (Blue and Purple Flowers)

1 columbine *(Aquilegia)*

1 mophead hydrangea *(Hydrangea macrophylla)*

1 bi-coloured grape hyacinth *(Muscari latifolium)*

2 drumstick primula *(Primula denticulata)*

1 'Georgia Blue' speedwell *(Veronica umbrosa)*

1. There are three containers to plant up for this display, which is why I have suggested allocating a day to finish everything. You can plant the containers in whichever order you prefer. Ensure there are a few holes in the bottom of the plastic planter insert before planting. If necessary, use an electric drill or hammer and heavy-duty nail to put a hole in the bottom (see page 34). Cover the base of the planter with a few drainage crocks.

2. Fill the plastic planter about two-thirds full with potting mix, incorporating some perlite or vermiculite to improve drainage, then position the largest plant (here the rhododendron) towards the back. Check that the top of the root ball is sitting just below the rim and add or remove potting mix, as required. Next, plant the columbine and saxifrage next to the rhododendron, ensuring the root balls of all the plants are level.

3. Fill any gaps between the plants with more potting mix and press the surface down gently.

4. Plant the stone urn and tall planter in the same way (but without using a plastic planter insert), arranging the plants in the containers first to check you are happy with the display before planting.

5. Position the three planters, water well and allow to drain.

Aftercare — Established mophead hydrangeas can be pruned in late winter or early spring. Simply cut out one or two of the oldest stems at the base to encourage the plant to produce new growth. Although you can remove the spent flower heads from mophead hydrangeas, it is a good idea to leave them on the plant over winter to provide the new buds emerging below with some protection against frost.

Tip — You can water in a special compound feed available from garden centres to maintain the gorgeous blue colour of the mophead hydrangea.

Difficult gardening

Late spring to summer

Full sun

*Moderate to
heavy watering*

*Feed weekly in the
growing season with
a general-purpose
fertiliser*

SUSPENDED SPHERES

Hanging baskets have rather fallen out of favour in recent years, but are ideal for adding a splash of summer colour to your outdoor space. If you only have a small balcony or courtyard, these spheres, made from two joined hanging baskets (see page 36), are easy to accommodate and sure to attract admiring comments – and questions! I spray-painted the baskets before planting, but you can leave the metal as it is if you wish. The planting is beautifully clean and simple, perfect for the neat little spheres. I suggest you create three spheres (odd numbers are always more pleasing to the eye) and hang them at different levels for maximum impact. Rather than packing in lots of plants, as is often the case with hanging baskets, I kept things simple. I chose an unusual salmon-coloured salvia and combined this with 'Emily Pink' dahlia, a profusely flowering plant that blooms throughout the summer, and 'Apollo Lovesong' cosmos. This is a pretty cottage-garden favourite with feathery foliage that adds a whimsical touch to the spheres.

Get the Look

What You Need

Two metal hanging baskets

Spray paint

Newspaper

Moss (available from garden centres and florists)

Black landscape material (for lining the lower basket)

Scissors

Potting mix

Wire cutters or pliers

Galvanised metal wire, 1 mm in diameter (for fixing the baskets together)

S-hooks and metal chains (for suspending the spheres)

Plants

1 'Apollo Lovesong' cosmos (*Cosmos*)

1 'Emily Pink' dahlia (*Dahlia*)

1 'Salmon Pink' salvia (*Salvia*)

1. In a well-ventilated room, or outside, spray-paint the two hanging baskets and allow to dry before planting. Place a few sheets of newspaper on your work surface when spraying.

2. You'll need to line the basket that will form the lower half of the sphere to retain the potting mix. Line with sheet moss first, then cut a circle from the piece of black landscape material with a few splits for drainage, so it will fit inside the moss lining.

3. Half-fill the basket with potting mix, then gently firm this down with your fingers.

4. Arrange the plants inside the basket – using a cosmos, dahlia and salvia in each sphere – and cover the root balls of the plants with potting mix. Add more potting mix to fill any gaps between the plants. The plants I've used are all upright-growers, so they don't need to trail over the edge as is usually the case for hanging baskets.

5. Take the upper half of the sphere and lower it carefully over the plants, teasing the flowers and leaves through the gaps in the basket – try to achieve an even spacing of plants.

6. Use wire cutters or pliers to cut short lengths of wire to join the two halves of the sphere. Bend and wrap the wire around the 'rim' of each basket to fix the two halves securely. I suggest using four equally spaced wires around the circumference of the baskets.

7. Suspend the sphere using S-hooks and metal chains, then water well and allow to drain.

Aftercare — Salvias, dahlias and cosmos
all respond well to deadheading, so remove
spent flowers regularly to promote
continuous flowering.

PROVENÇAL PASTELS

Difficult gardening
❀ ❀ ❀

Summer
☼

Full sun
☼

Moderate watering
◊ ◊

*Feed every two weeks
in the growing season
with a general-purpose
fertiliser*
�£

A palette of soft Provençal pastels can always be relied on to create a beautiful setting, even in the busiest urban garden. The mauves, lilacs and whites of the flowers in this display are certain to create a relaxing calm. This planting scheme contains two different types of lavender, so benefits from a heady scent, especially when watered. I selected large zinc planters for this scheme, so as not to introduce any jarring notes – the soft grey of the zinc complements the hues of the plants beautifully. The beige plumes of the grass, 'Karl Foerster', flower early in summer and then turn golden brown in autumn. The leaves create a graceful arch from the stem to give the scene a willowy nature when the wind blows. I also included some large gabions, as I love the natural forms of the pebbles. One houses a 'Wrinkled Blue' pittosporum, a large, imposing plant with pretty foliage and dark stems. Striking, elemental and textural, the gabions introduce another wonderful note, calling to mind pebbles on a seashore and relaxing on a beach. Bliss.

Get the Look

What You Need

3 large zinc planters, each about 60-90 cm (24-35 in) in diameter

Large gabion planter, about 60 x 60 x 60 cm (24 x 24 x 24 in)

Plastic planter with drainage holes (to fit inside the gabion planter)

Drainage crocks

Gravel, horticultural sand, perlite or vermiculite (to improve drainage)

Potting mix

Beach pebbles

Plants

1 English lavender (*Lavandula angustifolia*)

1 bellflower (*Campanula persicaria*)

3 white snapdragon (*Antirrhinum*)

2 'Karl Foerster' feather reed grass (*Calamagrostis x acutiflora*)

2 'Caradonna' Balkan clary (*Salvia nemorosa*)

1 white dahlia (*Dahlia*)

1 'Little Lady' English lavender (*Lavandula angustifolia*)

1 white mophead hydrangea (*Hydrangea macrophylla*)

1 'Wrinkled Blue' pittosporum (*Pittosporum tenuifolium*)

1. Decide which plants you would like in each zinc planter. The mauves, lilacs and white used in this scheme means you can group and blend the plants however you wish. For the purple-mauve planters, I combined English lavender, bellflower, Balkan clary and snapdragon in one and feather reed grass and the 'Little Lady' lavender in the other. The white-themed planter contains Balkan clary, hydrangea and snapdragon. I planted the pittosporum in the gabion planter.

2. Cover the hole in the bottom of each zinc planter with a few drainage crocks to prevent it becoming clogged with potting mix. Adding a few handfuls of gravel, or another suitable additive, will also improve the drainage (see page 34) – the planters are quite large and so need to drain well.

3. Fill the first planter two-thirds full with potting mix. Start with the largest plant, so you can build the display gradually. Place the plant in the planter, adjusting the level of the potting mix, as required, so the top of the root ball is about an inch below the rim.

4. Continue adding the other plants, ensuring all the root balls are level. Fill any gaps between the plants with more potting mix and firm in gently.

5. Repeat for the other planters, then water well and allow to drain.

6. For the gabion, I planted the pittosporum in a large plastic planter (with added drainage holes) that would fit inside the metal framework. I then placed the planter inside the framework and packed lots of beautiful beach pebbles around it. As the planter will be heavy, I suggest positioning it inside the cage first before planting.

Aftercare — Cut back the feather reed grass in early spring to promote healthy new growth and flowers. Prune English lavender in early autumn to promote strong growth the following season.

Tip — I love the large, concrete table and wire basket stools for entertaining. Along with the architectural garden spheres, they create a modern setting and really set the scene for a relaxing summer's day.

ENTRANCE TROUGHS

Medium gardening

Late spring to summer

Full sun to partial shade

Moderate watering

Feed every two weeks
in the growing season
with a general-purpose
fertiliser

A smart entranceway gives your property an instant update
and welcomes visitors to your home (including yourself).
These planters are quite traditional, but this formality is softened
by the relaxed approach to the planting. I did, however, make
sure the planting in each trough was more or less symmetrical.
I painted the troughs a glossy dark blue – the bright cerise flowers
in particular just sing against the gorgeous paint. As the name
suggests, the tall, frothy, aromatic fronds of 'Purpureum' bronze
fennel are similarly dark – these sultry plants add a mystic touch
to the display.

Get the Look

What You Need

2 formal troughs, about
45-60 cm (18-24 in) long
and 45 cm (18 in) deep

Deep blue gloss paint
(I used Farrow & Ball
Hague Blue)

Large paintbrush

Drainage crocks

Potting mix

Plants

2 'Purpureum' bronze fennel
   (*Foeniculum vulgare*)

4 pink snapdragon
   (*Antirrhinum*)

2 'Rose Barlow' columbine
   (*Aquilegiavulgaris* var
   Stellata)

2 'Lavella' dahlia
   (*Dahlia pinnata*)

2 dark pink aster (*Aster*)

2 dark pink 'Whirligig'
   African daisy
   (*Osteosperumum*)

2 Sweetunia Series 'Black
   Satin' petunia (*Petunia*)

1. Thoroughly clean the outside of the troughs (see page 34) first, as you want a nice, smooth surface for the gloss paint to adhere to. Give each trough two coats of paint, allowing the first coat to dry before applying the next. There is no need to paint inside the troughs – just the top part as the rest will be hidden by potting mix.

2. Cover the base of the troughs with a few drainage crocks, then fill two-thirds full with potting mix.

3. Start by planting the bronze fennel in the first trough, positioning it towards the back in the middle. Once you are sure the root ball is an inch or so below the rim of the trough, and added or removed potting mix as necessary, build up the display by planting the pink snapdragons on either side of the fennel.

4. Next, plant the columbine behind the fennel and, again, check the root balls of all the plants are nice and level.

5. Position the dahlia, with its bold pink flowers, in the middle of the trough, right at the front. This plant really needs to take centre stage.

6. Continue adding the remainder of the plants, filling in any gaps and placing the smaller petunias at the front.

7. Fill any gaps between the plants with more potting mix and firm in gently. Repeat for the other trough, trying to achieve as much symmetry as possible between the two planters.

8. Water well and allow to drain.

Aftercare — Regularly deadheading the petunias and dahlias will encourage the plants to produce more flowers through the summer.

Tip — Remove the seed heads of columbine if you want to prevent them self-seeding in your garden or containers. Or perhaps save the seeds and have a go at propagating them for more plants the following year.

PANTONE 'LIVING CORAL' PLANTERS

As I write, this container scheme is completely on trend as it uses the Pantone Colour of 2019 – Living Coral®. I used this vibrant shade to paint two trough planters and think it looks stunning against the soft grey backdrop. You could do this with any colour of the season for an on-trend look. The integrated bench supporting the planters is painted the same light grey – the overall effect is one of modern sophistication.

The planting is dominated by two colours: pink and dark purple, which complement but don't overpower the look of the planter. The light pink double flowers of Cinderella Series stock are wonderfully scented and long-lasting, making them a late-spring must-have, while the pretty pink flowers of 'Rubrifolia' thrift sit above dark copper-coloured foliage. This perennial is evergreen, which means the striking foliage will add some colour later in the year once the main flush of flowers is over. Cascading over the sides of the planters are the highly decorative, purple-black leaves of 'Trailing Black' morning glory, which contrast beautifully with the coral colour.

Get the Look

What You Need

2 trough planters, about
45-60 cm (18-24 in) long
and 45 cm (18 in) deep

Drainage crocks

Potting mix

Plants

4 Cinderella Series stock
(*Matthiola incana*)

4 'Apollo Lovesong' cosmos
(*Cosmos bipinnatus*)

1 'Trailing Black' morning
glory (*Ipomoea*)

1 'Rubrifolia' thrift
(*Armeria maritima*)

1. Cover the base of the planters with a few drainage crocks, then fill two-thirds full with potting mix.

2. Plant the larger specimens first – here, the stock and cosmos, positioning them before planting to check you're happy with the display. I included two of each plant in both planters, alternating them towards the back. Check the root balls of the plants are an inch or so below the rim of the planter, adding or removing potting mix, as required.

3. The plants with the dark foliage should sit at the front of the planter where they will contrast with the coral colour. So, plant the morning glory and thrift in front of the larger plants and check the levels as before.

4. Fill any gaps between the plants with handfuls of potting mix and firm in gently. Repeat for the other trough.

5. Water well and allow to drain.

Aftercare — Deadhead the flowers of all the plants in this display to encourage the production of new flowers.

Pantone 'Living Coral' Planters

The Projects   83

RED TROUGH

Medium gardening

Late spring
to late summer

Full sun to partial shade

Moderate watering

Feed weekly in the
growing season with
a general-purpose
fertiliser

The planting in this display is reminiscent of a cottage garden, but on a miniature scale. The combination of red, purple and pink hues creates a harmonious scheme that is enhanced by the rustic-looking planter, an old onion box that I have put to good use. The pinkish-red lupins are the central feature, their tall spires contrasting with the daisy-like flowers that make up the rest of the display. The African daisy is ideal for a bright sunny spot, being heat-tolerant – 'FlowerPower Red' is intensely coloured and also compact, making it ideal for growing in containers. The sophisticated, coral-red flowers of 'Embers Wish' salvia sit above pale olive-green leaves and bloom throughout the summer. Grown in the open garden, taller salvias may require some form of support, but are fine propped up by other plants in a container. I love the tantalising, purple-black, double flowers of the columbine, 'Black Barlow', with its wonderful fine foliage – the dark, sultry flowers are a real favourite of mine. The wonderful, clump-forming 'Roma' astrantia has pincushion flowers that are the colour of candy floss. They appear in late spring – just make sure you provide enough sunshine to bring out the full colour. Although this display will be at its best in late spring and summer, the trailing red flowers of verbena will happily bloom until early autumn.

Old reclaimed onion box,
about 50 x 40 x 30 cm
(20 x 16 x 12 in)

Electric drill or hammer
and heavy-duty nail

Black plastic sheeting,
(for lining the box)
(optional)

Staple gun and staples
(optional)

Drainage crocks

Potting mix

Plants

2 'Gallery Series Red'
  lupin (*Lupinus*)

1 'Embers Wish' salvia
  (*Salvia*)

1 'Roma' astrantia
  (*Astrantia*)

1 'Black Barlow' columbine
  (*Aquilegia vulgaris* var.
  Stellata)

1 'St Brigid Governor'
  garden anemone (*Anemone*)

1 'FlowerPower Red' African
  daisy (*Osteospermum*)

1 'Molly Sanderson'
  viola (*Viola*)

1 'Lanai Early Deep Red'
  verbena (*Verbena*)

1. As this container is recycled, you'll need to add some drainage holes to the bottom, either with an electric drill or a hammer and heavy-duty nail (see page 34). Then line the box with some black plastic sheeting, to prevent the wood rotting (see page 36). Ensure there are a few holes in the bottom of the sheeting before planting.

2. Cover the base of the box with a few drainage crocks, then fill two-thirds full with potting mix. Position the lupins in the box first as these are the key plants in the display. I used two lupins here, spacing them apart equally, but you could include more depending on the size of your box. Check the tops of the root balls are sitting an inch or below the rim of the pot and add or remove potting mix, as required.

3. Next, plant the other tall, upright plants – the salvia, astrantia and columbine – around the two lupins, ensuring the root balls of all the plants are level.

4. Fill in the gaps between the main plants with the smaller anemone, African daisy, viola and verbena. The idea is to pack the plants in quite tightly to create a feeling of abundance.

5. Fill any gaps between the plants with more potting mix and firm in gently.

6. Move the box into position, then water well and allow to drain.

Aftercare — The trick with this display is to cut back the foliage regularly so the jewel-reds of the flowers really pop. Deadhead the salvia and African daisy regularly to promote further flushes of flowers.

PASTEL TRIO

Medium gardening

Late spring to summer

Full sun to partial shade

Moderate watering

Feed weekly in the
growing season with
a general-purpose
fertiliser

Even if you only have a small courtyard or patio, there is scope for creating a mini garden by planting several large containers. Here, I chose three large planters in beautiful pastel shades and filled them with delicately coloured flowers to create a naturalistic display.

The tall, wand-like stems of 'Geyser White' gaura give the scheme a lovely airiness – this plant is also a real magnet for bees due to its nectar-rich flowers. I used two types of fuchsia – these are a great choice for containers or summer bedding schemes, having a long flowering time and always putting on a good show. I am particularly fond of 'Annabel' fuchsia. Its pendent double flowers, set above light green foliage, look stunning in shades of creamy white to pale pink, and they bloom continuously through summer and into autumn. It eventually forms an upright, half-hardy deciduous shrub. The trailing 'Happy Wedding Day' fuchsia has gorgeous, ruffled blush-white flowers with distinctive cerise markings. It looks striking with the silver foliage and white flowers of the shrubby bindweed.

The gazania is an interesting plant, creating a wonderful display in hot, sunny positions. The daisy-like flowers are available in various shades of red, pink, orange and bronze. When the weather turns dull, the flowers close up, but then open again as soon as the sun returns. Less showy, but equally striking, is 'Angel Wings' senecio with its large, velvety silver leaves. Although the small yellow flowers fade in summer, this evergreen perennial will supply interest all year round (although you may have to provide protection in winter). 'Zwartzkop' aeonium, with dark purple-black leaves, is an evergreen succulent that brings a touch of the exotic to any container scheme, although it is not hardy outdoors in winter. Position the planters in full sun, but bear in mind that plantain lilies require partial shade – tucking the lily in among the other plants should supply some respite from the sun.

Get the Look

2 large white galvanised metal planters, about 60 cm (24 in) tall and 50 cm (20 in) in diameter

1 medium white galvanised metal planter, about 45 cm (18 in) tall and 40 cm (16 in) in diameter

Blush-pink chalkboard spray paint (for the two large planters)

Electric drill or hammer and heavy-duty nail (optional)

Drainage crocks

Potting mix

Perlite or vermiculite (to improve drainage)

Plants

1 juniper (*Juniperus communis*)

5 'Geyser White' gaura (*Gaura lindheimeri*)

1 'Halcyon' plantain lily (*Hosta*)

3 'Annabel' fuchsia (*Fuchsia*)

3 'Happy Wedding Day' fuchsia (*Fuchsia*)

1 'Zwartzkop' aeonium (*Aeonium*)

1 shrubby bindweed (*Convolvulus cneorum*)

3 Daybreak Series (pink) gazania (*Gazania*)

1 'Goring Silver' everlasting flower (*Helichrysum petiolare*)

1 'Angel Wings' senecio (*Senecio candicans*)

1. Clean the outside of the two planters you are going to spray-paint (see page 32) and allow to dry thoroughly before spray-painting.

2. In a well-ventilated room, or outside, spray-paint the planters and allow to dry. Place a few sheets of newspaper on your work surface when spraying.

3. Cover the holes in the base of all three planters with drainage crocks. If necessary, use an electric drill or a hammer and heavy-duty nail to add a few drainage holes (see page 34).

4. Fill each planter two-thirds full with potting mix. I added some vermiculite to the potting mix to improve the drainage as some of the plants prefer a moist, but well-drained soil.

5. This scheme is very informal, so you can divide the plants among the three planters as you wish. However, I suggest using the juniper as a feature plant in one of the planters and splitting the gauras, fuchsias and gazanias among all three.

6. Start by planting the central plants – the juniper, gauras and plantain lily – ensuring the plants' root balls are sitting an inch or so below the rims of the planters. Adjust the level of the potting mix, as required.

7. Add the remaining plants, positioning the fuchsias towards the front, so their lovely flowers can trail over the sides. Check the root balls of the plants are level, as before.

8. Fill any gaps between the plants with more potting mix and firm in gently.

9. Position your planters, water well and allow to drain.

Aftercare — Although fuchsias are happy in full sun or partial shade, it is best to avoid hot afternoon sunshine. Trim the everlasting flower to keep it neat and tidy. If you wish, remove the insignificant flowers as they appear. Deadhead the gazanias for continuous blooms. Prune shrubby bindweed in the autumn to encourage bushiness. Cut back the gauras after they have finished flowering in the autumn. If you keep the 'Annabel' fuchsia to grow on as shrubs, they will need protection from cold, drying winds in winter. The senecio will also need some frost protection apart from in very mild areas. The aeonium can be grown outdoors in the summer in the UK, but will not survive the winter and temperatures below 5–10°C (41–50°F). If you wish, plant in a new container and bring indoors to enjoy as a houseplant.

Tips — If you'd like to attract wildlife into your garden, you'll find gazanias are a great choice for encouraging visits from butterflies. Fuchsias respond well to feeding. To encourage lots of flowers, choose a fertiliser containing plenty of potassium (often sold as a high-potash feed). The senecio can be brought indoors for the winter as a houseplant. Simply pot up in an individual container and bring inside before the first severe frost. Indoors, through winter, provide bright light and minimal water.

CORNER STORE

Easy gardening

Late spring to summer

Full sun

Moderate to heavy watering

Feed every two weeks in the growing season with a general-purpose fertiliser

A plant stand or *étagère* is a practical way to display container plants, particularly if you are short on space. Using the vertical dimension means you are not as limited in terms of the number of plants you can enjoy in a confined area. I used a mixture of containers here, although the stand-out stars are the beautiful traditional Bergs Potter pots. These are made from clay, which gives the roots of plants room to breathe and holds in moisture. The deep green of these Bergs pots sets the tone for a dark scene of black and pink flora. The delicate pale lavender flowers of 'Bishop of Leicester' dahlia, which have darker bands running down the middle of each petal, are delightful and especially good value because they flower into early autumn. However, the purple-black foliage of the morning glory and dahlia is key to the success of this display – it makes a real statement.

Get the Look

What You Need

Plant stand or étagère

A selection of containers in different materials, such as clay, metal and stone

Drainage crocks

Potting mix

Plants

1 Black-leaved dahlia
  (*Dahlia*)

1 'Bishop of Leicester'
  dahlia (*Dahlia*)

1 'Trailing Black' morning
  glory (*Ipomoea*)

1 Sweetunia Series 'Black
  Satin' petunia (*Petunia*)

1. Decide which plant you'd like in each container, perhaps arranging them in their plastic pots on the display stand first to see what works well.

2. Take your first container and add a few drainage crocks to the bottom to prevent the drainage holes becoming blocked with potting mix. Then fill the container two-thirds full with potting mix.

3. Place your chosen plant in its container and check the planting depth – the root ball should be sitting an inch or so below the rim. Add or remove potting mix, as required, to achieve the right level.

4. Add more potting mix to fill the gap between the plant and the sides of the container, then firm in gently.

5. Plant up the remainder of the containers in the same way, then lift them into position, water well and allow to drain.

Aftercare — Deadhead the plants in this scheme on a regular basis to ensure further flushes of flowers and to keep the plants looking tidy.

Tip — To protect the plant stand or étagère, you may want to place circular base trays beneath each container so water has something to drain into. Be inventive here. Try using items you already have at home, such as vintage plates or serving platters.

SWEET PEA TROUGH

Difficult gardening
◊ ◊ ◊

Summer
☼

Full sun
☼

*Moderate to
heavy watering*
◊ ◊ ◊

*Feed every two weeks
in the growing season
with a general-purpose
fertiliser*
✂

If you have a large expanse of wall or fencing, it just calls out to be adorned with a climbing plant – here, I planted a backdrop of 'Almond Pink Mrs Boulton' sweet pea for a selection of frothy pink flowers in a grey trough planter. The intoxicating fragrance of sweet peas is synonymous with summer; I just love them, and they can also be cut for a vase indoors. The metal grid supporting the sweet peas is a shop-fitting mesh panel that is available online and an inexpensive way to get a stylish trellis, as those specifically made for the garden can be expensive if you're looking for a contemporary design. I then filled the planter with snapdragon, diascia and coneflower – their pretty flowers in varying shades of pink look gorgeous with the grey of the planter and are perfect for a summer display. 'Diamond Light Pink' diascia is a very useful upright plant, having a vast number of delicate, pink flowers; it's great for pots and baskets.

Get the Look

Grey metal trough planter, about 70 x 50 x 30 cm (28 x 20 x 12 in)

Metal shop-fitting mesh panel, about 6 m (20 ft) tall and 60 cm (24 in) wide (to support the sweet peas)

2-4 large nails (for fixing the panel)

Electric drill or a hammer and heavy-duty nail (optional)

Drainage crocks

Potting mix

Sweet pea support rings or garden twine, for tying in the sweet peas (optional)

Plants

5 'Almond Pink Mrs Boulton' sweet pea (Lathyrus odoratus)

5 'Appleblossom' snapdragon (Antirrhinum majus)

1 'Diamond Light Pink' diascia (Diascia)

2 'Supreme Cantaloupe' coneflower (Echinacea)

3 orange-pink verbena (Verbena)

1. Position the trough planter against the wall or fence. Check the planter has drainage holes. If not, you can add these using an electric drill or a hammer and heavy-duty nail (see page 34). Cover the holes with drainage crocks.

2. Nail the mesh panel for training the sweet peas to the wall or fence, so the bottom is roughly level with the top of the planter.

3. Fill the planter two-thirds full with potting mix and plant the five sweet peas along the back so they will be able to climb up and over the panel. Although sweet peas are self-clinging climbers that will wind their tendrils around the supporting framework, it's a good idea to give them a helping hand by tucking some of the stems in place or tying them in with rings or garden twine. Make sure the root ball of each plant is an inch or so beneath the top of the planter and adjust the level of the potting mix, as required.

4. Add the remainder of the plants, positioning a coneflower at each end of the planter (just next to the edge of the panel) and a frill of diascia and snapdragon along the front.

5. Fill any gaps between the plants with more potting mix and firm in gently. Water well and allow to drain.

Aftercare — When growing sweet peas, keep tying in the new shoots as they clamber over the panel, especially if they are pointing outwards or look as if they may break. Sweet peas do not like to dry out, particularly when they are grown in pots, so ensure the water reaches the roots and water daily in hot, dry weather. Deadhead the sweet peas as often as possible. This is important for the annual 'Almond Pink Mrs Boulton', which will cease flowering if seedpods are allowed to develop.

Tips — If you love the scent of sweet peas, and want to try different varieties, be sure to choose annual ones because they have a stronger fragrance than their perennial cousins. The more you pick sweet peas, the more they grow. So, cut some as flowers for a vase and enjoy their gorgeous fragrance indoors, too.

MEADOW PLANTERS

Medium gardening

Summer

Full sun

Low to
moderate watering

Feed with a general-
purpose fertiliser
in spring

After visiting the Queen Elizabeth Olympic Park in London, I really wanted to have a wild meadow garden at home – no mean feat when all you have is pots. Fortunately, I came across a wonderful company called Pictorial Meadows who supply ready-made 'turf' containing wild-flower seed, giving you a lovely display of wild flowers. The wild-flower turf is easy to establish and hardly contains any grass (just 1 per cent) because this can quickly overwhelm the perennial flower species. Instead, the little meadow plants are grown in a special substrate. I simply cut the turf down to size to fit my pots. You can also buy seeds for sowing yourself, but I think the results can sometimes be hit and miss when growing wild flowers in containers.

Pictorial Meadows offer a range of turfs for different seasons, all of which contain a variety of beautiful wild flowers. I chose a summer-flowering mix that provides a burst of pink, white and blue (with some additional yellows). I particularly like the bright pink flowers of German pink and the architectural violet-blue flower spikes of viper's bugloss, which is a magnet for bees. Common yarrow has small, cream or pink flowerheads in summer, but the filigree foliage is also of note, giving a lovely texture to the display. You'll find that these wild-flower containers encourage bees, butterflies and other beneficial insects to your garden space.

Get the Look

What You Need

2 large stone pots, each about 45–60 cm (18–24 in) in diameter

Drainage crocks

Garden soil

Garden compost or potting mix

Fine gravel, horticultural sand, perlite or vermiculite (to improve drainage)

Your choice of wild-flower turf

Ruler

Gardening knife or sharp scissors

Plants

In the turf mix shown here:

Common yarrow
(*Achillea millefolium*)

German pink
(*Dianthus carthusianorum*)

Viper's bugloss
(*Echium vulgare*)

Hard fescue
(*Festuca longifolia*)

Lady's bedstraw
(*Galium verum*)

Common toadflax
(*Linaria vulgaris*)

Common cowslip
(*Primula veris*)

'Meadow Buttercup' ranunculus
(*Ranunculus aeris*)

1. Start by covering the holes in the base of the pots with drainage crocks.

2. Wild flowers prefer a poor soil with few nutrients, so it is best to use garden soil mixed with a little garden compost or potting mix to provide them with the best possible start. They also prefer well-drained soils, so I like to incorporate some fine gravel into the potting mix to improve drainage.

3. Fill the pots with potting mix until it is about 5 cm (2 in) from the top. The substrate on which the plants are growing is not very deep and you want to bring it near the rim of the pots.

4. Measure the diameter of the first pot, then cut the substrate down to size. You may need to cut the substrate slightly smaller so you can position it in the pot more easily.

5. Place the substrate gently in the pot, taking care not to damage the little plants. Check you are happy with the level and add or remove potting mix, as required. Push down gently so the roots of the plants come into contact with the potting mix beneath.

6. Repeat the process for the other container, then water well and allow to drain.

Aftercare — Deadhead the common yarrow, German pink, viper's bugloss and meadow buttercup regularly to promote further flowering. Common cowslip and common toadflax require deadheading to prevent them self-seeding everywhere and becoming invasive.

Tips — The flowerheads of common yarrow can be cut and dried for indoors. Avoid overwatering wild-flower containers.

PINK AND BLACK PLANTER

This is a truly beautiful display, with the subtle pink of the pot harmonising perfectly with the foliage of the morning glory and its gentle curves echoing the plants' heart-shaped leaves. The pot is made from terracotta and painted in Bauwerk Lime Paint in Malibu. This is a natural paint that has been specifically developed for most exterior wall surfaces, including cement, brick and render. It works best when it is absorbed into the wall, leaving a breathable surface that is protected by the natural properties of the paint. It is also ideal for terracotta pots because it allows the clay to breathe. The paint does not require an undercoat or sealer and can be applied immediately to both new and old surfaces. Morning glory are brilliant container plants, here trailing softly over the side of the pot. The leaves of this cultivar are as close to true black as possible. You don't need to add any more plants to a display such as this, the morning glory are just perfect on their own. They originate from warm parts of the world, so are sensitive to cold. For this reason, they are usually grown as an annual in more temperate climates. Position the pot in a warm, sunny, sheltered location – this bright corner of a courtyard is ideal.

Get the Look

1. Clean the outside of the pot (see page 32) and allow to dry thoroughly. Place a few sheets of newspaper on your work surface for painting.

2. Paint the pot with the blush-coloured paint – you don't need to paint the inside of the pot, just the top inch or so as the rest will be hidden by the potting mix. Allow the pot to dry thoroughly – this may take a while because terracotta is very absorbent.

3. Cover the hole in the bottom of the pot with drainage crocks.

4. Fill the pot two-thirds full with potting mix and arrange the morning glory on the surface. There are three plants, so position them in a triangular shape so they will fill the planter once established. Check the root balls of the plants are sitting an inch or so below the rim of the pot and add or remove potting mix, as required.

5. Fill any gaps between the plants with more potting mix and firm in gently.

6. Place the pot on the pot feet in your chosen location, then water well and allow to drain.

Aftercare — Cut back or remove the stems of the morning glory to keep the plants tidy, as necessary.

BLUE AND YELLOW PLANTER

Easy gardening

Summer to mid-autumn

Full sun to partial shade

Moderate watering

Feed every two weeks in the growing season with a general-purpose fertiliser

This pretty planter, with its relaxed blue and yellow blooms, brings to mind a pretty cottage garden overflowing with flowers. The Bert & May floor tiles, in geometric blue and white, make the perfect platform for the display. The plants I chose have flowers that are simple and unassuming, perfect for an informal container, and include the beautiful, lavender-blue flowers of 'Blue Note' scabious – I love the frilly delicacy of this compact little perennial. I especially like the mauve-blue double flowers of the petunias and the daisy-like brachyscome tumbling flamboyantly over the side of the planter.

The yellow element is provided by three BeautiCal 'Caramel Yellow' petchoa. Petchoas are a recent hybrid between two genera: Petunia and Calibrachoa. This particular cultivar has sunshine-yellow flowers with orange-brown centres and veining on the petals. Petchoas are ideal plants for beginner gardeners, being easy to grow and having good rain tolerance – the petals are less prone to unsightly marks in wet weather. The golden yellow, daisy-like flowers of the gaillardia are also worthy of note. Although happy in full sun, some of these plants tolerate partial shade, making this scheme ideal for a sunny courtyard that is in shade for part of the day.

Get the Look

What You Need

Large galvanised metal planter (I used an old dustbin), about 40 cm (16 in) tall and 50 cm (20 in) in diameter

Electric drill or hammer and heavy-duty nail (optional)

Drainage crocks

Potting mix

Perlite or vermiculite (for drainage)

Plants

1 'Fairy Queen' mealy cup sage (*Salvia farinacea*)

1 'Green Trick' sweet William (*Dianthus barbatus*)

1 'Mesa Yellow' F1 Hybrid Blanket flower (*Gaillardia*)

1 'Blue Note' scabious (*Scabiosa japonica*)

3 BeautiCal 'Caramel Yellow' petchoa (*Petchoa*)

3 Tumbelina 'Maria' petunia (*Petunia*)

2 'Blue' brachyscome (*Brachyscome multifida*)

1 'Mesa Yellow' F (*Gaillardia x grandiflora*)

1. Start by covering the holes in the bottom of the planter with drainage crocks. If necessary, use an electric drill or a hammer and heavy-duty nail to add a few drainage holes to the base (see page 34).

2. Fill the planter two-thirds full with potting mix. I incorporated some vermiculite into the potting mix to improve drainage because some of the plants prefer a moist, but well-drained soil.

3. Start by planting the taller plants – the mealy cup sage, sweet William, gaillardia and scabious – towards the back of the planter. Make sure the root balls of the plants are sitting an inch or so below the rim and adjust the level of the potting mix, as required.

4. Add the remaining plants, positioning the petchoa in the middle towards the front. Make sure the petunia and brachyscome are planted at the edge of the planter so they can tumble over the side once established. You are trying to create a feeling of frothy abundance. Check the root balls of the plants are level, as before.

5. Fill any gaps between the plants with more potting mix and firm in gently.

6. Position your planter, water well and allow to drain.

Aftercare — Deadheading regularly will ensure more flowers through the season. These plants will flower into the autumn, so deadheading is definitely worth the effort. Give the brachyscome a light trim if it starts to look untidy.

Tips — Sweet William makes a fantastic cut flower that will last over a month in a vase.

Half-day project

NEON POT

Easy gardening

Summer

*Full sun
(avoid hot midday
sun for geraniums)*

Moderate watering

◊◊

*Feed every two weeks
in the growing season
with a general-purpose
fertiliser*

✂

Brightly coloured geraniums are perfect for sunny locations, putting on a good show throughout the summer. This makes them ideal for summer containers, especially if there is a likelihood that you will be less than vigilant with the watering. Bear in mind, however, that although most cultivars prefer sunny conditions, they should be shaded from very hot sun.

This scheme of hot, vibrant colours also includes lime-green coleus (this may be labelled Solenostemon) and sunshine-yellow 'Double Zahara Yellow' zinnia – it really does live up to its name: Neon Pot. It just sings of sunny climes and Mediterranean holidays. Zinnias make brilliant container plants and always provide reliable colour. Like most perennials grown in containers or as summer bedding, geraniums are tender, so the pot should not be planted up and left outside until all risk of frost has passed – usually towards the end of May in the UK. The planting scheme does not rely solely on vibrant flowers, however, since the geraniums belong to the Zonal Group, which means their leaves have attractive markings, while the green leaves of the coleus are ribbed and textured.

Get the Look

1. Cover the hole in the bottom of the pot with drainage crocks.

2. Half-fill the pot with potting mix and plant the taller yellow zinnia and dahlia toward the back. Check the plants' root balls are sitting an inch or so below the rim of the pot and add or remove potting mix, as required.

3. Next, plant the two geraniums in front of the zinnia and dahlia. As they grow, they will bush out and the pretty scalloped leaves will soften the edge of the pot. Lastly, I tucked the coleus in at the side.

4. Again, check all the root balls are level, fill any gaps between the plants with more potting mix and firm in gently.

5. Position the pot in a warm, sunny spot, water well and allow to drain.

Aftercare — Keep deadheading the geraniums, and you will enjoy more flowers through the season. Geraniums are perennials, although they are often grown as annuals and disposed of at the end of the summer. However, it's possible to overwinter them for planting again the following spring. There are various ways to do this, but the most practical one, especially if you only have a few specimens, is to plant them in individual plastic pots and keep them in a light, well-ventilated, frost-free place. Make sure the plants aren't touching each other, too. Water sparingly (the best time is in the morning) when the plants show signs of wilting, and ensure the water can drain from the pots.

Tip — Many people love coleus for their foliage and think they look their best before flowering, so pinch off the flowers when they appear if you wish.

SCREENING WALL

Difficult gardening

*Summer to
early autumn*

Full sun

Moderate watering

*Feed every two weeks
in the growing season
with a general-purpose
fertiliser*

Slatted trellising painted a subtle shade of grey-blue is ideal for screening and disguising a large expanse of brick or concrete wall. Any type of trelliswork calls for embellishment with a climber to soften the effect and enhance the space. Here, I used star jasmine, a pretty evergreen climber with creamy, highly scented star-shaped flowers that bring a touch of the exotic to any scheme. You also have the added benefit of glossy dark-green leaves that often turn dark red in winter. Star jasmine prefers shelter from cold winds, making it an ideal plant for a display in an enclosed courtyard. The velvety flowers of chocolate cosmos – named for their delicious chocolate scent – bring a rich and sumptuous tone to this large-scale planting display. The deep chocolate-red flowers of 'Chocamocha' have an even more pronounced chocolate scent. Equally enticing is 'Sea Breeze' fleabane, which produces masses of mauve daisy-like flowers with large yellow centres throughout the summer, making this perennial perfect for a feature planter such as this. I love the rustic beauty of COR-TEN steel planters, but they can be expensive. Here, I used a fibre-glass planter and applied a rust-effect paint. I then coated the planter with a rust activator, which will add a layer of rust. It will gradually get rustier over time – at a fraction of the cost.

Get the Look

What You Need

Large fibre-glass trough planter, about 80 x 50 x 30 cm (31 x 20 x 12 in)

Rust-effect paint (I used Craig & Rose Artisan Copper Effect)

Rust activator

Large paintbrush

Large trellis panel, with wide slats, about 2.4 m x 80 cm (7½ ft x 2½ ft)

Plastic Rawlplugs, large screws and an electric drill (to fix the trellis panel to the wall)

Spirit level

Electric drill or hammer and heavy-duty nail (optional)

Vine eyes and coated metal wire (for training the climber)

Drainage crocks

Potting mix

Plants

1 'Velocity Blue' salvia star jasmine (*Trachelospermum jasminoides*)

1 'Chocamocha' chocolate cosmos (*Cosmos atrosanguineus*)

1 'Sea Breeze' fleabane (*Erigeron karvinskianus*)

1 'Velocity Blue' salvia (*Salvia*)

1 large 'Little Lady' English lavender (*Lavandula angustifolia*)

1 'Supreme Cantaloupe' coneflower (*Echinacea*)

1. Clean the outside of the trough planter (see page 32) and leave to dry thoroughly before painting.

2. Paint the planter with the rust-effect paint and allow to dry thoroughly before coating with the activator (follow the manufacturer's directions carefully). You'll need to protect the surface you are working on with newspaper.

3. Fix the trellis panel to the wall. Pre-drill the panel and mark the corresponding holes on the wall. Drill the holes in the wall and insert a Rawlplug in each one. Then, screw the panel to the wall. Use the spirit level to check the panel is level.

4. Add some drainage crocks to the bottom of the planter. If necessary, use an electric drill or a hammer and heavy-duty nail to add a few drainage holes (see page 34).

5. Fill with potting mix until it is about two-thirds full. Plant the star jasmine on the left towards the back of the planter so you will be able to train it over the trellis panel. Make sure the root ball is an inch or so below the top of the planter, adjusting the level of the potting mix, as required.

6. Screw vine eyes into the trellis panel, spacing them evenly so you can train the star jasmine up and across the panel. Thread the vine eyes with the wire – I crossed a couple of lengths of wire across the panel to provide a secure framework – and gently train the stems of the climber over the panel. You are aiming to create a fan shape.

7. As the planter is not very deep, I suggest planting the remaining plants more or less in a row. Working from left to right, I planted the chocolate cosmos, fleabane, salvia, English lavender and coneflower. Remember to check all the plants' root balls are level and add or remove potting mix if necessary.

8. Fill any gaps between the plants with more potting mix and firm in gently. Water well and allow to drain.

Aftercare — Star jasmine requires shelter from cold, drying winds, so it is best to grow this climber against a wall that faces south, south-west or west.

Tips — If you wish, you can use masonry screws to fix trellis panels directly to a wall without having to use Rawlplugs – this is a good idea if you want to save time. When attaching trellis panels to a wall, you might want to fix wooden battening to the wall first (using plastic Rawlplugs and screws), then screw the trellis to the battening. This creates a larger gap and so greater airflow behind the plants.

Screening Wall

Half-day project

RUSTIC STEEL

Medium gardening

_Summer to
early autumn_

Full sun

Moderate watering

_Feed every two weeks
in the growing season
with a general-purpose
fertiliser_

Made from COR-TEN steel, this incredible planter is very large and makes a real statement in any outdoor space. Due to its size, I didn't fill it completely with potting mix. Instead, I placed plastic plant pots in the base to fill some of the space first.

The planting has a lovely, cottage-garden feel, but with a modern edge. Delphiniums, for example, are mainstays of the cottage garden, but can need staking in the open garden. Here, however, I used a compact cultivar from the perennial Magic Fountains Series, which have dense flower spikes in white or shades of purple and blue. 'Lollipop' verbena is a dwarf cultivar of the familiar tall-growing species, making it another ideal choice for container planting. The large, pinkish-purple, thistle-like flowers of globe artichoke put on a fantastic display into early autumn, looking beautiful among the feathery stems of 'Karl Foerster'. This tall grass forms the architectural backbone of the planting – in fact, a striking container such as this calls for a powerful star plant.

Although the colour scheme is based around purple, mauve and pink, the black foliage of 'Black Pearl' coral flower ticks all those dark, sultry boxes. Truly black plants are few and far between, but the coral flower's prettily scalloped, nearly black leaves look stunning against the steel.

Get the Look

What You Need

Large COR-TEN steel
planter, about 80 cm
(31 in) in diameter

Plastic plant pots
(to fill the base
of the planter)

Drainage crocks

Potting mix

Plants

1 'Karl Foerster'
   feather reed grass
   (Calamagrostis x
   acutiflora)

3 'Magic Fountains Lilac
   Rose' delphinium
   (Delphinium)

1 'Lollipop' verbena
   (Verbena bonariensis)

1 'Chocamocha'
   chocolate cosmos
   (Cosmos atrosanguineus)

1 globe artichoke
   (Cynara cardunculus)

1 'Black Pearl' coral
   flower (Heuchera)

1 'Caradonna' Balkan clary
   (Salvia nemorosa)

1 'Ulster Dwarf Blue'
   veronica (Veronica Spicata)

1. Position your planter first, as it will be very heavy once planted. Cover the drainage hole in the bottom with a few crocks. Being such a large planter, there may be more than one to cover.

2. Put some plastic plant pots upside down in the bottom of the planter, to fill up the space and reduce the amount of potting mix you need.

3. Fill the planter with potting mix until it is about 30 cm (12 in) from the top. Begin by planting the large grass. As I positioned the planter against a wall, I planted the grass towards the back. Check the root ball of the grass is an inch or so below the rim of the planter and adjust the level of the potting mix, as required.

4. Next, plant the other taller plants, such as the delphiniums and verbena, in front of and around the grass. Check the root balls are level, then plant the smaller plants towards the front and edge of the planter. You want to pack the plants quite tightly to create the effect of an abundant cottage garden.

5. Fill any gaps between the plants with more potting mix and firm in gently. Water well and allow to drain.

Aftercare — The feather reed grass will remain a feature of the scheme long after the flowers have faded. Once the grass is established, cut back old stems in early spring to the level of the potting mix before new growth starts again. Deadhead the delphiniums by cutting the spent flower spikes back to small flowering side shoots. Cut down all growth to the level of the potting mix once the plants have died back in the autumn. Remove old and unattractive foliage from the coral flower in spring to allow new shoots to emerge.

Tip — Do not let the potting mix dry out as a few of the plants – the veronica, delphinium, coral flower and cosmos – prefer a moist, but well-drained soil.

PINK AND PURPLE PLANTER

Easy gardening
◿

Summer to autumn
☼ ⚘

Full sun
☼

Moderate watering
◊◊

Feed every two weeks
in the growing season
with a general-purpose
fertiliser
⚘

The deep rich tones of the pink and purple flowers look
stunning against the shiny metal planter and the soft grey
of the decking. The unusual pale blue glass spheres sitting
alongside bring a contemporary feel to the display, too. The star
of the show is undoubtedly the 'Atropurpurea Group' purple
beech – a deciduous tree with smooth, grey bark and gorgeous
purple leaves that retain their colour well into autumn before
sometimes turning reddish. I underplanted the beech with a
combination of upright perennials and annuals (my filler plants):
Archangel® 'Raspberry' angelonia, Sonata Series 'Carmine'
cosmos and 'Robin' purple loosestrife. The rose-pink flower
spikes of the purple loosestrife are particularly impressive and
very attractive to bees – in fact, beekeepers in North America
grow this plant because of its abundant, nectar-rich flowers. The
delicate, filigree foliage of the cosmos provides a gentle contrast
to the bold upright forms. Plants such as cosmos and angelonia
are also ideal for a sunny corner, being drought-tolerant and
happy in full sun.

Get the Look

1. As this is a large planter, I advise putting it in position first before filling with potting mix and planting up. If necessary, use an electric drill or a hammer and heavy-duty nail to add a few drainage holes (see page 34).

2. Fill the planter two-thirds full with potting mix. The purple beech, cosmos and brachysomes prefer moist, but well-drained soil, so it is worth incorporating some perlite or vermiculite into the potting mix to improve drainage, especially as the beech tree will be a permanent planting.

3. First, plant the beech tree in the middle of the planter – this is your thriller or focal plant, which will provide interest well into autumn after the summer flowers have faded. Ensure the root ball is an inch or so below the top of the planter, adjusting the level of the potting mix, as required.

4. Next, add the taller plants – the angelonias, cosmos and purple loosestrife – around the central beech tree, again checking you are happy with the planting level and adding or removing potting mix if necessary.

5. Plant the brachyscomes at the front of the planter, where their lovely flowers can trail down over the side. Check you are happy with the planting level and adjust, as required.

6. Fill any gaps between the plants with more potting mix and firm down gently. Water well and allow to drain.

Aftercare — Deadhead the angelonia, brachyscome and cosmos regularly to promote further flowering. If you wish, deadhead the purple loosestrife to prevent it self-seeding.

Tip — Although purple beech can be grown in a large container, it is a large tree that will need replanting in the garden at some stage. If you don't have a garden, then perhaps offer the tree to a friend.

BALCONY DISPLAY

If you have a large balcony, then suspending window boxes from the surrounding railings frees up valuable space, while also providing you with screening and privacy. Simply plant enough window boxes to line the balcony and add some much-needed greenery to your outdoor area. When installing window boxes at higher levels, it is important to ensure the fixings are secure and that there is no possibility of them falling and injuring anyone below (see page 36 for advice on fixing window boxes).

Although the plants in these window boxes are largely annuals, the Mexican fleabane is a perennial that will come back the following year. The highly perfumed Cinderella Series stock is available in shades of purple, mauve, pink and white, and is perfect on balmy summer evenings. Here, I chose cream and white to tie in with the design scheme. The line of window boxes is flanked by two large evergreen plants: a New Zealand flax and pittosporum in large olive oil jars that I painted cream. These provide year-round architectural interest and colour – the New Zealand flax with deep purple-black, sword-shaped leaves and the pittosporum with glossy, blue-grey leaves with wavy edges and dark stems. These add some permanence to the display, but you can easily ring in the seasonal changes by planting the boxes in autumn with a display of spring-flowering bulbs, such as white tulips and hyacinths.

I painted the window box fronts in Farrow & Ball French Gray, the same colour as my bookshelf indoors, to continue the theme outside on the balcony. The cool black-and-white colour scheme is reflected in the white bistro table and accompanying black chairs, as well as the outdoor rug with its striking diamond pattern.

Get the Look

What You Need

2 large terracotta olive oil jars

4 wooden window boxes, about 80 x 12 x 12 cm (31 x 5 x 5 in), or enough to fit your balcony space

Scrubbing brush or similar

Cream chalk paint, for the oil jars (I used Annie Sloan Cream)

Grey paint, for the window boxes (I used Farrow & Ball French Gray)

2 large paintbrushes

Electric drill or a hammer and heavy-duty nail (optional)

Window box brackets

Drainage crocks

Potting mix

Plants

For Each Window Box

2 white and/or cream Cinderella Series stock (*Matthiola incana*)

6 small white snapdragon (*Antirrhinum*)

1 large white cosmos (*Cosmos*)

2 'Trailing Black' morning glory (*Ipomoea*)

1 'Profusion' Mexican fleabane (*Erigeron Karvinskanius*)

For the Two Large Planters

1 'Wrinkled Blue' pittosporum (*Pittosporum tenuifolium*)

1 'Platt's Black' New Zealand flax (*Phormium*)

1. Clean the outside of the two olive oil jars (see page 32) and leave to dry thoroughly. Brush down the window boxes with a stiff brush – you want nice, clean surfaces for painting.

2. Paint the jars with the cream paint and allow to dry thoroughly before planting. Place a few sheets of newspaper on your work surface when painting.

3. Paint the window boxes with the grey paint and, again, allow to dry before planting.

4. I planted the jars first, covering the hole in the bottom of each with some drainage crocks. Fill the jars two-thirds full with potting mix, then plant the pittosporum in one and the New Zealand flax in the other. These are your two specimen plants. Make sure the root ball of each plant is an inch or so beneath the rims of the jars, adjusting the level of the potting mix, as required.

5. Fill the gap between the sides of the jars and the specimen plants with more potting mix and firm in gently.

6. Next, plant up the window boxes, covering the holes in the bases with a few drainage crocks first. If necessary, use an electric drill or a hammer and heavy-duty nail to add a few drainage holes (see page 34). It is advisable to fix the window boxes in position before filling them with potting mix and planting. Follow the directions provided by the manufacturer of the brackets carefully when fixing them in place.

7. To create a repeating pattern along the length of the balcony, plant each window box in roughly the same way. I planted the taller plants – here, the stocks, snapdragon and cosmos – at the back of the boxes. The smaller plants, the morning glory and Mexican fleabane, are planted at the front, so they can trail over the edge.

8. Fill any gaps between the plants with more potting mix and firm in gently. Water well and allow to drain.

Aftercare — Remove dead and damaged leaves from the New Zealand flax in spring. Both the flax and pittosporum may need protection from strong or cold winds in some areas, so ensure your balcony is well sheltered. Deadhead the Mexican fleabane to encourage further flushes of flowers.

Tips — The two white jars are very large and will be heavy when filled with potting mix and watered. Always make sure that the space you are positioning planters of this size – in this case, a balcony – can support their weight. If you are unsure, seek professional advice. Bear in mind that Mexican fleabane will attract pollinating bees and butterflies. It can also self-seed and pop up in the crevices of walls.

TERRACOTTA POT

For this display (on the left), I chose a lovely pale terracotta pot to provide a subtle stage for the gentle green, cream and light brown tones of the plants. The Mexican feather grass in particular puts on a magnificent display from early summer to autumn. A deciduous grass, it has soft, wispy leaves and airy plumes of flowers that turn a soft golden brown as summer progresses. Although ideal for a sunny garden, this grass can also be grown successfully in a large container. I love it for the sounds and movement it creates as the flowerheads drift in the breeze – it's also wonderful to run your fingers through the flowers.

Being deciduous, the Mexican feather grass does die back each year in autumn before new growth appears again the following spring. For this reason, I think the real star of the show here is evergreen 'Kirkii' hebe, with its glossy, spear-shaped leaves and long, white flowers in summer, because it provides interest all year round. Interestingly, it is considered a natural hybrid between two hebe species and was discovered in New Zealand by Thomas Kirk – hence the name. Hebes do not require a lot of care and attention once established, so this is a great container display if you are short on time. Further colour is supplied by the chocolate cosmos. This perennial appeals to all the senses: the deep crimson flowers have a velvety texture and smell deliciously of a box of chocolates.

Get the Look

What You Need

1 pale terracotta pot, about 35 cm (14 in) in diameter and 40 cm (16 in) tall

Drainage crocks

Potting mix

Perlite or vermiculite (to improve drainage)

Plants

2 'Kirkii' hebe (Hebe)

1 'Ponytails' Mexican feather grass (Stipa tenuissima)

1 'Chocamoca' chocolate cosmos (Cosmos astrosanguineus)

1. Cover the hole in the bottom of the pot with drainage crocks to prevent it becoming clogged with potting mix. I added some perlite/vermiculite to the potting mix to improve the drainage as these plants prefer a well-drained soil.

2. Fill the pot two-thirds full with potting mix. Plant the two hebe first – positioning them towards the front of the pot. Check the root balls of both plants are sitting an inch or so below the rim of the pot, adding or removing potting mix, as required.

3. Add the Mexican feather grass next, planting it just behind the hebe so the delicate flowerheads can arch elegantly above them. Finally, plant the cosmos in front of the hebe – this fills the space at the edge of the planter nicely and provides some further colour when in flower.

4. Check the root balls of all the plants are level and fill any gaps with more potting mix if required. Firm in gently.

5. Position the planter, water well and allow to drain.

Aftercare — Deadhead the hebe regularly to ensure further flushes of flowers. If you wish, trim the hebe all over in early winter to keep the plants healthy and tidy. Cut back the leaves of the Mexican feather grass in early spring before the new foliage starts to emerge.

Tips — The Mexican feather grass does not like to sit in wet potting mix, so ensure you provide ample drainage and water sparingly in winter. Although hebes are happy in sun or partial shade, the Mexican feather grass and cosmos require full sun to thrive, so place the pot in a sunny spot for the best results.

COTTAGE GARDEN PLANTER

This planting scheme is based on a combination of shades of pink, creating a subtle display that recalls a cottage garden. The planting is enhanced by the gorgeous peony colour of the Bauwerk paint on the wall – it really does help to show off the lovely late-summer blooms. I used a Fermob basket as a container here. Fermob baskets are unusual in that they have two holes with plugs at each end of the tray to let the water out. The soft apricot foxgloves are perfect for this scheme, adding a strong vertical accent above the other plants – this compact variety is perfect for growing in a container. The flat, pink achillea flowers will attract bees and other beneficial insects to your garden space, while the daisy-like echinacea provides abundant flowers with long-lasting colour throughout the summer. Look out for the changing colour of the echinacea flowers. They start as creamy yellow buds that become a rich pink as they mature before fading to a soft blush-pink. The perennial *Salvia* 'Kisses and Wishes' also has a long flowering period, the candy-pink flowers appearing in mid-summer and providing colour well into the autumn. It is a brilliant filler plant for containers or borders. I have suggested keeping this planter in a sunny location, although foxgloves are also happy in partial shade.

Get the Look

What You Need

Large fermob basket
or alternative planter,
approx. 30 cm (12 in)
tall and with a volume
of 50 litres (11 gallons)

Drainage crocks

Potting mix

Plants

1 'Summer Berries' yarrow
  (*Achillea millefolium*)

1 'Sunseekers Salmon'
  coneflower (*Echinacea*)

3 'Dalmation Peach'
  F1 Hybrid foxglove
  (*Digitalis purpurea*)

1 'Kisses and Wishes'
  salvia (*Salvia*)

1 English lavender
  (*Lavandula angustifolia*)

1. Cover the holes in the bottom of the basket with drainage crocks.

2. Fill the basket two-thirds full with potting mix. I planted the foxgloves first, positioning them in a triangle in the basket – these are your thriller plants. Check the rootballs of the plants are level and sitting an inch or so below the rim of the basket. Add or remove potting mix, as required.

3. Plant the filler plants next, here the achillea and echinacea, adding them among the foxgloves to create attractive levels. Finish by planting the two salvia cultivars around the edge of the planter.

4. Check the rootballs of all the plants are level and fill any gaps with more potting mix. Firm in gently.

5. Position the basket, water well and allow to drain.

Aftercare —Deadhead the salvias regularly to promote more flowers through the season.

BLUE PLANTER

Easy gardening

Summer to autumn
(NB the eucalyptus
is evergreen)

Full sun

Moderate watering

Feed every two weeks
in the growing season
with a general-purpose
fertiliser

The soft colours and shapes of this display are perfect for later in the year. I painted the planter a beautiful shade of blue (using Bauwerk Lime Paint), which really sets off the dark blue/purple hues of the plants. The ornamental kale and young eucalyptus plants are a great choice here, their rounded leaves complementing the curves of the planter perfectly. The blue juvenile foliage of evergreen cider gum is stunning and provides year-round appeal. Eucalyptus are fast-growing trees and shrubs, so I suggest you use these plants to add height to containers for a season, then transplant them in the open garden to grow into larger plants. This species of eucalyptus has small clusters of white flowers in summer and develops peeling cream and brown bark as the tree matures.

The leaves of ornamental kale always make a powerful statement; grown as an annual, these plants provide structure as well as beautifully shaded, slightly wavy foliage – so striking are the leaves that they look like large, exotic flowers. I also love the coleus cultivar used here: the gorgeous purple foliage is tinged with bright magenta in the middle and provides a perfect backdrop for the kale leaves. This coleus is also highly tolerant of pollution, making it an ideal container choice for those gardening in urban areas.

Get the Look

What You Need

1 round Fibreclay planter, about 50 cm (20 in) wide and 30 cm (12 in) tall

Bauwerk's Wild Duck Lime Paint

Large paintbrush

Drainage crocks

Potting mix

Plants

8 Acephala Group 'Purple Pigeon' ornamental kale (*Brassica oleracea*)

3 cider gum (*Eucalyptus gunii*)

2 'Black Dragon' coleus (*Coleus*)

1. Clean the outside of the planter (see page 32) and allow to dry thoroughly before painting. This may take a while as terracotta is very absorbent, which is why I have suggested you may need a weekend to finish this project.

2. Apply two coats of the blue paint, allowing the first to dry before applying the second. There is no need to paint the inside of the planter – just the top part – as the rest will be concealed by the potting mix. Place a few sheets of newspaper on your work surface when painting. Allow the paint to dry before planting.

3. Cover the hole in the bottom of the planter with drainage crocks.

4. Fill the planter two-thirds full with potting mix. Start with the largest plants – in this case the ornamental kale – positioning them at the front of the planter. Check the plants' root balls are sitting an inch or so below the rim of the planter, adding or removing potting mix, as required.

5. Plant the three eucalyptus in the middle of the planter and then add the tall coleus towards the back. Imagine that you are creating layers of foliage so all the beautiful colours and textures are on display.

6. Check the root balls of all the plants are level and fill any gaps with more potting mix. Firm in gently.

7. Position the planter in a sunny location, water well and allow to drain.

Aftercare — Make sure the potting mix does not dry out, as eucalyptus prefers a moist, but well-drained soil. For the best young foliage, cut the eucalyptus back in early spring to two or three buds above the base. Pinch out the young shoots of the coleus regularly to maintain a neat shape and the colour of the foliage.

Tip — I used young eucalyptus plants here, which are perfect as a filler plant for containers. To grow on to a larger bush or tree, plant them in a bigger pot on their own or move to the open garden.

SUCCULENT TROUGH

Medium gardening
◖ ◖

All year round
☼ ♦ ❋ ❀

Full sun
☼

*Moderate watering
(using the soak-and-
dry-out method)*
◊ ◊

*Feed once a month in
the growing season with
a liquid houseplant feed
or specialist liquid
cacti feed*

There is something very striking about the forms and colours of succulents, and they bring real elegance to a container. Using a trough or window box to grow these wonderful plants, rather than the more traditional round stone bowls, gives them a modern look. This planter was originally grey, but I wanted to set off the succulent's beautiful pastel shades, so I sprayed it with blackboard paint for a matte look. You could just as easily buy a black planter if you find one you like.

I have given this display a medium level, not because it is difficult to plant, but because watering succulents can be tricky and involves some trial and error. My advice would be to plant a few containers first before tackling this one. If you do experience failure, don't become despondent – I have had a few not go quite as planned, but you will learn from your mistakes. The finished trough, I'm sure you'll agree, is definitely one of extravagant beauty.

Get the Look

What You Need

Trough planter, about
60 cm (24 in) long

Black chalkboard
spray paint

Drainage crocks

Cacti and succulent
potting mix (for
extra drainage)

Plants

1 'Blue Canna' crassula
  (*Crassula*)

3 'Echoc' echeveria
  (*Echeveria*)

1 Mexican gem (*Echeveria
  elegans*)

1 Echeveria palinodes
  (*Echeveria palinodes*)

1 Moonstone (*Pachyphytum
  oviferum*)

3 Houseleeks (*Sempervivum*)

Note — I have provided the names of the
succulents used here, but don't worry too much
about using the exact varieties as availability
varies at garden centres. Just make sure you buy
the plants from the outdoor section to ensure
they are hardened off.

1. Clean the outside of the planter (see page 32) and allow to dry thoroughly before spray-painting. In a well-ventilated room, or outside, spray-paint the planter and allow to dry before planting up. Place a few sheets of newspaper on your work surface when spraying.

2. Cover the holes at the bottom of the planter with a few drainage crocks to prevent them becoming clogged with potting mix. Succulents love good drainage, and the roots don't like to become waterlogged.

3. Fill the planter with potting mix, so the root ball of the largest succulent will be sitting just below the rim. I like to work out the planting depth by placing the plastic pot next to the planter to see how much potting mix to use.

4. Take the succulents out of their plastic pots and arrange them in the planter until you are happy with your display.

5. If there are any small bare areas, you can break off small flower florets from the succulents – as long as they have a root – and use these to fill in the gaps.

6. Once you are happy with the arrangement, fill any gaps between the plants with more potting mix and firm in gently. Ensure you retain the gap at the top of the planter, so water doesn't run over when you water and splatter potting mix everywhere.

7. Water the planter thoroughly until you see water running out of the bottom, and allow to drain.

Aftercare — Let the planter dry out between waterings – the time period will differ depending on the season. Succulents will need more water during the growing season. Remove any dead foliage that falls from the plants, so it doesn't rot and cause disease. Bring the planter indoors if the weather dips below 10°C (50°F). Planters in a sheltered, south-facing position, however, should be fine. If you bring the planters inside, position them by a window, but not in direct sunlight as this will scorch the leaves.

Tip — Succulents need excellent drainage, so make sure your trough has sufficient drainage holes or drill or puncture a number of holes if you're using a recycled container (see page 34). If you don't have any specialist cacti and succulent potting mix, I recommend adding fine gravel, horticultural sand or another suitable additive (see page 28) to make standard potting mix more free-draining. If the leaves of the succulents start looking shrivelled, then they need more water. If they are looking translucent, then you are overwatering.

HANGING AND GROUND TURQUOISE PLANTERS

To me the contrast between the turquoise of the planters and the green foliage of the ivy and ferns is just stunning, joining together perfectly, especially in a shady corner or perhaps on a balcony or roof garden. I got the idea for this planter while sitting in a restaurant. They had suspended window boxes containing houseplants from the ceiling, so I adapted the idea. You could indeed suspend these planters from a ceiling, but be careful that they are secured firmly. If you don't have much outdoor space, then a simple bench for the ground planter and a metal grille from which you can suspend the hanging planter makes a powerful statement – simple, chic and eye-catching.

I used ferns and trailing ivy in the hanging planter and Hart's tongue fern in the ground planter. The strap-shaped leaves of this fern are a beautiful emerald-green, giving a wonderful display, especially during winter. Both the ivy and ferns are evergreen, meaning that these planters will provide a low-maintenance display throughout the year. Please note: although ivy can tolerate full sun, Hart's tongue is a woodland fern that prefers shade and should be kept out of direct sunlight.

As one of the planters is suspended, make sure the material from which it is made is light enough to hang up when filled with potting mix. I had these made in fibre glass, which is a great lightweight material. You can get these in any Pantone colour you wish (I chose turquoise) – make sure you ask the supplier to add drainage holes for you.

Get the Look

2 fibre-glass window
boxes, about 90-120 cm
(35-47 in) in length

Electric drill or hammer
and heavy-duty nail
(optional)

Drainage crocks

Potting mix

About 1 m (3 ft) of brass
chain (for suspending the
hanging planter)

4 keyrings or S-hooks

Plants

For the Hanging Planter

6 small trailing ivy, such as
  'Mein Herz' (Hedera helix)

2 medium soft shield fern
  (Polystichum setiferum)

For the Ground Planter

3 Hart's tongue fern
  (Asplenium colopendrium)

1. Ensure both planters have drainage holes. If not, use an electric drill or hammer and heavy-duty nail to add a few holes to the bottom (see page 34), but bear in mind that fibre glass can be difficult to drill.

2. Cover the holes with drainage crocks and half-fill the planters with potting mix. Arrange the ivies and ferns in the hanging planter and the Hart's tongue ferns in the ground planter, ensuring the tops of the root balls are sitting an inch or so below the rims.

3. Fill any gaps between the plants with handfuls of potting mix, then firm in gently.

4. Suspend the hanging planter – here I used chains to suspend the planter from a metal grille using S-hooks.

5. Lift the hanging planter into position before watering, or it will be very heavy to move. Water both planters and allow to drain.

Note — Turn to page 37 for guidance on how to suspend the hanging planter.

Aftercare — Remove dead and unsightly fronds from the ferns before the new leaf tips start to unfurl. It's also a good idea to clear away any debris that accumulates between the fronds to maintain good air circulation.

EVERGREEN SALMON PLANTER

This stately planter provides a year-round display, making it very useful for a front/back entrance or doorstep. The salmon-coloured planter complements the emerald-green of the plants beautifully – these evergreens also have leaves in contrasting sizes, which adds a textural element to the display. Made from galvanised metal that I spray-painted salmon-pink, the planter looks deceptively like a real terracotta pot. The planting is very simple, using only two types of plant: Japanese laurel and spindle tree.

The Japanese laurel, 'Rozannie', is a neat evergreen shrub with glossy, dark green leaves. The foliage of this good-value plant provides year-round interest, but it also has lovely, dark red-purple flowers in spring followed by large, bright red berries. Being long-lived, it is perfect for a permanent planting and a great container choice near a busy road as it is tolerant of urban pollution. The spindle tree at the front of the planter has a slow growth rate, making it ideal for long-term container growing – in many ways, it is a good alternative to box, having similar evergreen foliage, while not being susceptible to the dreaded box blight. I trimmed the spindle tree level to create a mini-hedge in front of the aucuba – I think this works well and produces a pleasing formality.

Get the Look

What You Need

Galvanised metal planter,
about 50 cm (20 in)
in diameter and 60 cm
(24 in) tall

Salmon-pink spray paint

Electric drill or hammer
and heavy-duty nail
(optional)

Drainage crocks

Potting mix

Plants

1 'Rozannie' Japanese
  laurel (Aucuba japonica)

4 small 'Green Spire'
  spindle tree (Euonymus
  japonicus)

1. Clean the outside of the planter (see page 32) and allow to dry thoroughly before spray-painting.

2. In a well-ventilated room, or outside, spray-paint the planter and allow to dry before planting. Place a few sheets of newspaper on your work surface when spraying.

3. Cover the holes in the base of the planter with drainage crocks. If necessary, use an electric drill or a hammer and heavy-duty nail to add a few drainage holes (see page 34).

4. Fill the planter two-thirds full with potting mix. First, I planted the specimen plant, in this case the Japanese laurel, in the middle of the planter. Check the plant's root ball is sitting an inch or so below the rim of the planter and adjust the level of the potting mix, as required.

5. I surrounded the Japanese laurel with a mini-hedge by planting the four spindle trees around the edge of the planter. Again, ensure the root balls of the spindle trees are sitting an inch or so below the rim. Adjust the level of the potting mix, as required.

6. Fill any gaps between the plants with more potting mix and firm in gently.

7. Position the planter, water well and allow to drain.

Aftercare — Prune out straggly branches from the Japanese laurel in spring if you'd like to encourage bushy growth and then feed after pruning to promote new foliage. Even with regular pruning, this plant grows quickly and can live for a long time. Trim the branch tips of the spindle tree in late spring and again in early autumn if required.

Tip — Using a high-nitrogen feed will promote strong foliage growth in container-grown shrubs.

Half-day project

EVERGREEN PLANTERS FOR DOORWAYS

Easy gardening

All year round

Full sun or partial shade

Moderate watering

Feed monthly in the growing season with a general-purpose liquid feed

A pair of clipped box plants on either side of a front door always looks smart and has a more traditional look. Being evergreen, the box also provides year-round interest, which is perfect for a permanent planting such as this. This scheme is a celebration of the wonderful palette of greens that plants can provide, from the luscious dark green of the ivy and box to the brighter green of the grasses. Although clipped box plants lend architectural formality to a planting, here this is softened by the swaying wispiness of the grasses.

I chose the perennial 'Hameln', a cultivar of Chinese fountain grass with pretty, purple-tinged flowers in late summer. The leaves are bright green, turning yellow in autumn and then slowly fading to brown through the winter. Cascading over the edge of the planters is Irish ivy, a sumptuous ivy with large, dark green leaves and small, yellowish-green flowers that are followed by black berries in winter. I love the large-leaved lobes of Irish ivy as they are much softer than other ivies. All in all, this planter is perfect if you are looking for an easy, low-maintenance scheme to embellish the entrance to your home all year round.

Get the Look

What You Need

2 dark grey Fibreclay planters, each approx. 49 x 60 x 30 cm (19 x 24 x 12 in)

Drainage crocks

Potting mix

Plants

2 common box, about 30 cm (12 in) in diameter (*Buxus sempervirens*)

4 'Hameln' Chinese fountain grass (*Pennisetum alopecuroides*)

4 medium trailing ivies, such as Irish ivy (*Hedera hibernica*)

1. Cover the holes in the base of the planters with drainage crocks. The Chinese fountain grass, in particular, prefers a well-drained potting mix.

2. Fill the planters two-thirds full with potting mix. Plant the box plants first, as these are the central feature of the display, placing one in the middle of each planter. Check the root balls of the plants are sitting an inch or so below the top of the planters, and add or remove potting mix, as required.

3. Plant two Chinese fountain grass on either side of each box plant, then slip the trailing ivies around the edge of the planters so their leaves can trail down over the sides.

4. Again, check the root balls of all the plants are level, fill any gaps with more potting mix and firm in gently.

5. Position the planters on either side of your front door – or at the end of a path – water well and allow to drain.

Aftercare — Water the planters regularly, as box plants do not like to dry out. Make sure the potting mix is kept moist, but not waterlogged, even in the winter. Box is susceptible to a range of problems, including box blight, so keep an eye out for signs of distress such as leaf spots, stem dieback and bare patches, and treat accordingly. The box tree moth can be particularly devastating, as the caterpillars can defoliate plants completely. As a precaution, I spray my box plants every couple of weeks with a bug killer and this seems to safeguard them from infestation. If the plants do succumb, either remove the caterpillars by hand or spray the plants with an appropriate commercial bug killer every week at times of the year when the caterpillars are prevalent – look out for white webbing among the leaves, which houses the developing pupae. Trim the box plants to maintain their shape in mid- or late summer. If you would like the plants to look very neat and precise, then they can be clipped twice a year: once in early summer and then again in late summer or early autumn.Remove the dead foliage and old flowering stems from the Chinese fountain grass in the spring. Box plants can benefit from a high-potash feed to avoid discoloration of the leaves, which can easily be mistaken for box blight (rather than a potash deficiency). Fertilisers specially formulated for box are available.

Tips — If you plan to grow shrubs such as box in a container permanently, then top-dress established plants in spring with fresh potting mix and a little slow-release fertiliser. The Chinese fountain grass may need some frost protection in the winter in colder areas. You can use Japanese holly instead of box as it can be clipped to a similar shape and isn't affected by box caterpillar.

One-day project

OMBRÉ HERB POTS

Easy gardening
🌿

All year round
☼ ❀ ❄ ❁

Edible
🍴

Full sun
☼

Moderate watering
◊ ◊

Feed every two weeks
in the growing season
with a general-purpose
fertiliser (half
recommended dose)
✿

There is nothing better than picking fresh herbs for cooking, knowing that you've personally grown an ingredient for your dishes. Even if you have a large garden with space for a herb bed, the ease of just popping outside to grab a sprig of rosemary is very appealing – especially in winter. The warmth of the ombré pink tones used to paint these terracotta pots really complements the fresh green hues of the herbs and turns the humble terracotta pot into something special. Potting herbs separately has the added benefit that you can grow a selection of herbs with different watering requirements, which you can't accommodate in one pot. Here, I used emulsion paint in varying shades of pink to create the ombré effect, but you could just as easily use your favourite colour in different tones.

Get the Look

What You Need

6 small terracotta pots
in different shapes,
about 12-15 cm (5-6 in)
in diameter

6 different shades of
non-toxic emulsion paint
in one colour

6 tester brushes (one
for each shade to speed
up painting time)

Drainage crocks

Gravel (to improve drainage)

Potting mix

Plants

Mint (*Mentha*)

Thai basil (*Ocimum
tenuifolium*)

Marjoram (*Origanum
majorana*)

Rosemary (*Rosmarinus
officinalis*)

Sage (*Salvia officinalis*)

Thyme (*Thymus officinalis*)

1. Clean the pots (see page 32) well before painting and planting, especially if you have used old pots, as I have here. Allow to dry thoroughly.

2. Paint each pot a different shade of your chosen colour. Give each pot two coats of paint, allowing the first coat to dry before applying the next. There is no need to paint inside the pots – just the top part as the rest will be hidden by potting mix.

3. Before planting, match each herb to the most appropriately sized pot, ensuring the plants will have room to grow.

4. Cover the hole in the bottom of each pot with a drainage crock to prevent it becoming clogged with potting mix. I also added a few handfuls of gravel to improve the drainage (see page 34).

5. Half-fill the pots with potting mix and position the first herb in its new pot. Once the herb is planted, the surface of the potting mix should be about an inch below the rim of the pot to allow for watering, so adjust the planting depth by adding or removing potting mix as necessary.

6. Fill around the root ball with more potting mix and firm in gently. Repeat for the remaining pots.

7. Water the pots and allow to drain. If you wish, add a layer of gravel to the top of the pots. Not only does this add a nice decorative finish but it also helps retain moisture.

Aftercare — The more you pinch off sprigs from the herbs, the more the plant will produce. Mint, marjoram and sage will need more water than the hardier herbs in this display. So, if you see any wilted, droopy leaves, provide more water. In the winter, you can move the pots indoors to a sunny window.

Tip — Avoid planting mint in a mixed container because it is an aggressive grower and can take over a planter. If you would like to combine mint in a container with other plants, keep it in its plastic growing container.

Half-day to one-day project

SHADY PLANTERS

Easy gardening

Autumn · winter · spring

Shade

Heavy watering

Feed every month in the growing season with a general-purpose fertiliser

I have a tricky corner in my garden that doesn't get much sun and looks rather bare. I wanted to create an abundant display for most of the year, which can prove difficult in shady areas like these. So, I selected shade-loving plants, displaying them in two faux concrete planters to give an industrial feel that juxtaposes with the greens of the foliage. The deep emerald-green of the moss is so attractive and in the bleak months really lifts my spirits. The moss is also a great holding plant before brighter blooms are available, without you having to plant up a whole container. Just ask a local florist to get two boxes of moss for you or visit your local flower market.

Ferns are the oldest living plants, with more than ten thousand varieties, and act as great oxygenators that filter the air. They also provide a touch of drama as their beautiful curling fronds unfurl – the copper shield fern used here is also hardy in winter. Japanese aralia is a wonderful, big, bold plant that gives you a lot of bang for your buck. It is also easy to maintain – albeit requiring a little pruning. This is a really easy display, although it takes a bit of time and effort to get the moss tightly fitted on the surface of the moss planter.

Get the Look

What You Need

2 large planters, both
about 60-90 cm (24-35 in)
in diameter

Drainage crocks
(for the larger planter)

Potting mix

Floristry pins

Plants

Bun moss and pincushion
moss (*Leucobryum glaucum*)

1 Japanese aralia (*Fatsia
japonica*)

1 'Brilliance' copper
shield fern (*Dryopteris
erythrosora*)

1 'Purpurea' spurge
(*Euphorbia amygdaloides*)